Walch Toolbook Series

Drama: A Comprehensive Guide to Dramatic Elements and Style

Clark Stevens

J. WESTON

WALCH

PUBLISHER

Portland, Maine

User's Guide
to
Walch Reproducible Books

As part of our general effort to provide educational materials that are as practical and economical as possible, we have designated this publication a "reproducible book." The designation means that purchase of the book includes purchase of the right to limited reproduction of all pages on which this symbol appears:

Here is the basic Walch policy: We grant to individual purchasers of this book the right to make sufficient copies of reproducible pages for use by all students of a single teacher. This permission is limited to a single teacher and does not apply to entire schools or school systems, so institutions purchasing the book should pass the permission on to a single teacher. Copying of the book or its parts for resale is prohibited.

Any questions regarding this policy or requests to purchase further reproduction rights should be addressed to:

Permissions Editor
J. Weston Walch, Publisher
321 Valley Street • P.O. Box 658
Portland, Maine 04104-0658

1   2   3   4   5   6   7   8   9   10

ISBN 0-8251-3916-3

Contents

Part 4: Stage Tools—Elements of Play Production . . . 95

Appendices 109

To the Teacher

As part of the Walch **Toolbook** series, *Toolbook for Drama* has been prepared as a comprehensive, reproducible encyclopedia of basic concepts involved in appreciating—and enjoying—the dramatic arts.

The goal of this publication is to provide teachers with a variety of teaching tools and approaches to excite students who are learning about drama.

The term "drama" is used here in its broadest sense. For our purposes, both serious and comic dramatic material are classified as "drama." In addition, though a majority of these teaching aids has been targeted specifically to the study of stage drama, an attempt has been made throughout to extend concepts to other media popular with students, particularly film and television drama.

These materials have been written to provide students with a solid grounding in all elements of drama, including the history of drama, critical vocabulary, and elements of theatrical production. They have been conceived to help students develop critical skills that can be applied to appreciating classical drama as well as popular entertainment.

In addition to analytical activities, a variety of suggested creative follow-up activities have also been included to invite students to appreciate the craft of drama "from the inside." **A Reading List of Great Plays** offers suggestions for extended classroom or independent study.

Format

The *Toolbook for Drama* is divided into four main parts. Each part begins with a brief section called Teacher Notes. This section provides an overview of the themes covered in that part, teaching tips, a warm-up exercise, and ideas for possible extension activities.

Each part also contains a series of short, reproducible readings on elements of the topic. Following each reading, you will find reproducible student activity pages designed to help students personalize, as well as amplify, ideas introduced in the specific reading.

Part 1: Introduction to Drama introduces students to the origins and history of Western drama, and includes a reading on drama in non-Western cultures. The last two readings invite students to look at similarities and differences among the three dramatic media of today: live theater, film, and television. Throughout, students are encouraged to think about their own past and present experience of dramatic performances.

Part 2: Basic Tools—Elements of Drama introduces students to six core elements of drama: Conflict, Character, Dialogue, Setting, Plot, and Dramatic Structure. Included in the follow-up activities are opportunities for student dramatists to struggle with the same issues of craft that have faced dramatists throughout the history of drama.

Part 3: Other Dramatic Tools—Appreciating Plays as Literature first offers suggestions for students faced with the task of bringing a play script "to life" in the imagination when read on the page. Students are then introduced to critical skills involved with analyzing drama as literature: imagery and symbolism, themes and ideas, and categories of dramatic genre (tragedy, melodrama, comedy, satire, and farce).

Part 4: Stage Tools—Elements of Play Production focuses on aspects of play production. Readings deal with the skills and training required of actors, the many tasks of the stage director, and the contributions made behind the scenes by other key participants. Some follow-up activities allow students to "try on" aspects of these creative roles.

In addition, five Appendices have been included. You will find a master list of **Drama Vocabulary** that includes definitions of key concepts introduced in the text; a reproducible handout for student drama critics entitled **Tips for Reviewing a Dramatic Performance**; a **Playscript Format and Playscript Sample** and a **Screenplay Format and Screenplay Sample**, offered as models for students who wish to compose their own stagescripts or screenplays; and a list of resources **Recommended for Further Reading**.

Ways to Use This Toolbook

These materials have been designed for flexible use according to individual teacher needs. Since school curricula vary so widely, neither the student readings nor follow-up activities have been specifically keyed to the intensive study of any particular play.

In addition, you may choose to use the reproducible reading or follow-up activity pages of an entire unit (or the whole book) in sequence, or to use them selectively according to your specific classroom needs.

For instance, specific reproducible materials—say, on topics such as Character, Setting, or Plot—might be introduced to students just before beginning to study a play, before attending a play as a class, during the study of a play, or before staging a play production. In the same way, any follow-up activity could also be used as a stand-alone activity.

Teaching Drama in the Classroom

All too often, students (and actually some teachers, too!) find themselves dreading the drama unit of their curriculum. How do you reach students who think they "hate" drama?

Many students dislike studying drama because drama seems irrelevant to their personal lives. "Boring old plays" studied as literature can't compete with the flashy entertainment of television and film. For other students, reading plays feels like too much hard work. The more accessible pleasures of watching TV programs or popular films seem much easier.

Studying drama may also seem foreign to students who have little experience attending live theater performances. Shy students, too, may feel inhibited about participating in performance-related activities in the classroom.

Ultimately, there is no magic way to win over reluctant students, whatever the source of their resistance. However, here are some thoughts that may be helpful.

First of all, try to encourage an open and honest climate in your classroom. Listen, and take your students' reactions seriously. An honest reaction is where true appreciation starts.

To my mind, adolescents have an absolute right to think Shakespeare is "boring" until we do our job of convincing them, with good evidence, that he isn't. Play texts are by nature "living" texts that must be brought to life anew for each new audience. Approaching any play—even one by an acknowledged genius—as "sacred" is the surest way to kill it for your class.

Second, it's important to sympathize with your students when they find it difficult to stage a play in their minds while reading it on the page. Encourage a whole class discussion about the problems involved. Perhaps the more accomplished students may have some good advice to share with others.

Third, address the "relevancy" issue head-on. What *does* Oedipus' situation have to do with us? It's an intellectually honest question. What discussions can you lead to blow the dust off what may seem truly like ancient history?

One strategy might be to invite students to find parallels in the dramas they already know and care about—film and TV. Another might be to encourage students to talk about parallels they find with their own life experience. Throw out an open-ended question such as "When have *you* felt caught in a situation in which you felt that fate was against you? How did *you* feel?"

Fourth, wherever possible, stop just *talking* about plays. Find ways for your students to bring drama to life in your class.

Are there classic and/or contemporary videos in your school or town library? Can you videotape samples of drama from present-day television programming (old movies? soap operas? sitcoms?)? Any form of drama can be grist for the mill.

Also, how about inviting your students to perform pieces of drama texts in class—as well as improvising drama? Books of theater games are readily available. Take some risks yourself, too—it may bring your students closer to you as you all join together in the fun.

Another related idea is to encourage students with a creative writing bent to write their own scenes (even whole plays) to be staged and performed by others in the class. Find drama-related activities that tap the particular strengths of your non-academic students. For instance, get "artistic" students working on scene design and "class clowns" working on comedy skits.

You will find a number of possible activities described in the pages that follow. It is my hope that they will fire your own imagination, too, to find ways to "sell" a truly great product—drama—to your class.

Reading List of Great Plays

This list offers a source for teachers looking for suitable "great play" texts to use with their classes. Many of these plays have the added benefit of being available in video format for possible classroom viewing.

Chronological Survey of Western Drama

Aeschylus	*Agamemnon* *The Libation Bearers* *The Eumenides*
Sophocles	*Oedipus The King* *Oedipus at Colonus* *Antigone*
Euripides	*Medea*
Aristophanes	*The Birds*
Anonymous	*The Second Shepherds' Play* (from the Wakefield Mystery Cycle)
Anonymous	*Everyman*
Christopher Marlowe	*Dr. Faustus*
William Shakespeare	*Henry IV, Part I* *Julius Caesar* *The Merchant of Venice* *Romeo and Juliet* (possible tie-in to *West Side Story*) *Macbeth* *A Midsummer Night's Dream* *As You Like It* *Much Ado About Nothing*
Pierre Corneille	*Le Cid*
Jean Racine	*Phèdre*
Molière	*The Imaginary Invalid* *The Miser*
Oliver Goldsmith	*She Stoops to Conquer*
Edmond Rostand	*Cyrano de Bergerac* (possible tie-in to film *Roxanne*)
Oscar Wilde	*The Importance of Being Earnest*

Henrik Ibsen	*The Wild Duck* *A Doll's House*
August Strindberg	*A Dream Play* *Miss Julie*
Luigi Pirandello	*Six Characters in Search of an Author*
Anton Chekhov	*The Cherry Orchard*
George Bernard Shaw	*Pygmalion* (possible tie-in to *My Fair Lady*) *Saint Joan* *Arms and the Man*
John M. Synge	*The Playboy of the Western World*
Bertolt Brecht	*The Good Woman of Setzuan* *Mother Courage and Her Children*
Jean Paul Sartre	*No Exit*
Eugene Ionesco	*The Bald Soprano* *The Lesson* *Rhinoceros*
Samuel Beckett	*Waiting for Godot*
Dario Fo	*Accidental Death of an Anarchist* *Can't Pay? Won't Pay!*

Twentieth-Century American & British Dramatists

Eugene O'Neill	*Ah, Wilderness!* *The Hairy Ape* *The Iceman Cometh* *A Long Day's Journey Into Night*
Thornton Wilder	*Our Town*
Clifford Odets	*Awake and Sing!*
Carson McCullers	*The Member of the Wedding*
Arthur Miller	*The Crucible* *Death of a Salesman*
Tennessee Williams	*The Glass Menagerie*
Edgar Lee Masters	*Spoon River Anthology*
Reginald Rose	*Twelve Angry Men*
Jerome Lawrence & Robert E. Lee	*Inherit the Wind* *The Night Thoreau Spent in Jail*
Lorraine Hansberry	*A Raisin in the Sun*
Edward Albee	*The American Dream* *The Zoo Story*

William Gibson	*The Miracle Worker*
Frances Goodrich & Albert Hackett	*Diary of Anne Frank*
Robert Bolt	*A Man for All Seasons*
Harold Pinter	*The Birthday Party*
Robert Anderson	*I Never Sang for My Father*
Peter Shaffer	*The Royal Hunt of the Sun* *Amadeus* (possible tie-in to film)
Tom Stoppard	*Rosencrantz and Guildenstern Are Dead*
Joseph Heller	*We Bombed in New Haven*
Lonne Elder	*Ceremonies in Dark Old Men*
Mark Medoff	*Children of a Lesser God*
Athol Fugard	*Master Harold . . . and the Boys*
Edward Sacamoto	*In the Alley*
Frank Chin	*The Chickencoop Chinamen* *The Year of the Dragon*
Neil Simon	*Brighton Beach Memoirs* *Broadway Bound*
Wing Tek Lum	*Oranges Are Lucky*
Luis Valdez	*Zoot Suit*
Sam Shepard	*True West*
August Wilson	*Fences*

Part 1:
Introduction to Drama

Objectives

1. To introduce students to the rich history of Western and non-Western drama;

2. To promote the special qualities of live drama;

3. To link stage drama to drama as it is produced in the popular media of film and television.

Teaching Tips

Teachers will find it useful to validate each student's own experiences with drama. Wherever possible, help your students to link new learnings with past experience—work toward the unknown (i.e., Bunraku puppet theater) from the known (i.e., Jim Henson's Muppets™ and other puppet creations).

The follow-up activities can be fitted to each student's learning style to assure success. These activities range from academic research-based assignments to hands-on experiments and performance opportunities.

Audiovisuals quickly bring ideas alive when other approaches fail. Use supplementary audiovisual materials wherever possible: recordings, overhead projections of illustrations from books and periodicals, audio recordings, films and videotapes, etc.

Warm-up Activity

From its earliest origins, ritual and drama have been designed to appeal to many senses. In the 1960s, theater groups produced intimate theatrical "Happenings" designed to stimulate all the senses of the audience—simultaneously.

To help your students appreciate the "aliveness" of live theater, break your class into small groups of four students to plan and execute a three-minute, simultaneous, multi-sensory "Happening" for other members of the class.

Encourage each group to include ideas intended to reach all five senses:

1. <u>sound</u>: (e.g., voices, musical instruments)

2. <u>sight</u>: (e.g., bright colors, masks, dancing, juggling)

3. <u>smell</u>: (e.g., perfumes, food smells)

4. <u>touch</u>: (e.g., passing around objects with different textures)

5. <u>taste</u>: (e.g., giving out foods with different tastes)

(continued)

Part 1:
Introduction to Drama *(continued)*

Extension Activities

- <u>Research the History of Theater Spaces</u>
  Over its 2,500 year history, Western drama has been shaped by a remarkable diversity of performing spaces. Invite your students to learn more about one or more of the following performing spaces: the Greek amphitheater; the theater for Roman comedy; the role of the pageant wagon in Medieval Mystery plays; the street theater of the Italian commedia dell'arte; Shakespeare's Globe Theater; the theater of Molière; or the proscenium theater of nineteenth-century and twentieth-century drama.

- <u>Commercials as Television "Drama"</u>
  Because television commercials must communicate a complex message in no more than one minute, makers of commercials tend to make use of striking visual and sound techniques to catch the viewer's attention. If possible, have students record and study a favorite commercial. Have them describe what techniques are used and why they believe them to be effective.

- Have students design and make (or illustrate on a poster) a prop for one of the theater styles described in this section, such as a model Greek theater, a mask, a pageant wagon, etc.

Name _____ Date _____

What Is Drama?

Have you ever seen a dramatic performance? How about children's theater, puppet shows, magic acts, plays at your school? These are all dramatic performances.

Now add to these all the films and television shows you have seen: sci-fi, horror films, cartoons, favorite TV series . . .

Give yourself credit. You already know a lot about drama! In a way, you've been a "drama critic" for a long time—talking about what you liked or disliked about performances you have seen.

This book will help you expand on what you already know. It will introduce you to concepts that will help you appreciate your experience of drama. You will also learn vocabulary to help you express what you think and feel.

What do we mean when we use the term "drama?" In your local video store the label "drama" is often used to describe movies that are "serious," as opposed, for instance, to the term "comedy."

This book will be using the term "drama" more broadly. For the ancient Greeks, the inventors of drama as we know it today, the word "drama" meant "to do" or "to act." A **drama** is simply a story—*any* story—that is acted out in front of an audience.

Defined in this way, drama can be serious or comic. Most of the time we will be focusing on drama as it is performed on the stage. But this definition applies to drama written for film and television as well.

Why do audiences enjoy watching drama? Think for a moment about the different kinds of drama that *you* enjoy.

Probably you have watched a live play performance, a film, or TV program that has moved you or had a lasting effect on you. Maybe it made you feel sad, or perhaps even made you cry.

Other times, you've chosen dramas that you knew would make you laugh, such as your favorite situation comedies on television. When you are tired or in a bad mood, the right comedy can make you feel better almost instantly.

Besides having an effect on your mood, what else can you get from watching drama? Well, some dramas are designed to transport you to a time and place that is quite unlike your own. How much have you learned about other parts of the country or the world by watching dramas—whether on stage, screen, or TV—that are set elsewhere?

How much have you learned about other periods of history, too? Like a time machine, drama can take you back (or forward) in time or to other cultures that are far different from yours. Whether it's a Greek tragedy, a biographical film about Abraham Lincoln, or a TV show such as *Dr. Quinn: Medicine Woman*, drama can take you out of your own world to a far different time.

Even when it doesn't take you to a different place or time, drama always allows you that special opportunity to step into the personal lives of other characters. It offers you the chance to be "a fly on the wall" in other people's lives. You meet characters who are far different from you—and surprisingly similar as well! We learn a great deal about ourselves in the process.

Name _____ Date _____

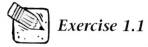 *Exercise 1.1*

Personal Drama Viewing

Directions: You have seen many examples of drama. Use the questions below to remind you of viewing experiences of drama. Draw from serious and comic dramas that you have viewed—on stage, film, or television.

1. Estimate (roughly) the number of dramas you have seen in the last 12 months:

   Stage plays _____

   Feature films viewed at movie theaters _____

   Feature films viewed at home on VCR _____

   Television dramas (weekly series, sitcoms, made-for-TV movies) _____

2. Think about all the serious dramas you have seen. Name one that had a lasting impact on you. Explain how it affected you.

   Title _____

   _____

   _____

3. Think about all the comic dramas you have seen. Name one that made you laugh. Explain what elements made it funny.

   Title _____

   _____

   _____

4. Name a drama you have seen that was set in another place or time. Tell what it taught you about a period of history or culture different from yours.

   Title _____

   _____

   _____

5. Name a drama you have seen that taught you something new about how people think and behave. Explain how this was important to you.

   Title _____

   _____

   _____

Name _____   Date _____

 *Exercise 1.2*

Remembering Your First Appearance Onstage

Even if you don't think of yourself as an "actor," many people have been in a play at least once in their lives.

Directions: In the space below, describe what you remember about your first experience on stage. What do you remember about: the play you were in? where it was performed? the part you played?

Who watched the play? What was it like for you to perform in front of an audience? In what ways has this early experience influenced your feelings about the study of drama?

_____

_____

_____

_____

_____

_____

_____

_____

_____

_____

_____

_____

_____

_____

_____

_____

_____

_____

_____

Drama: A Comprehensive Guide
to Dramatic Elements and Style

Name _____   Date _____

The Roots of Drama

Primitive Ritual

Modern drama has ancient roots. For primitive peoples, drama was rooted in sacred **ritual**. It had an extremely practical purpose. The earliest peoples acted out activities that were important to them in drama before actually engaging in them.

An ancient dance

For instance, before an actual hunt, one member of the tribe might pretend to be the animal to be hunted. Others would act out the roles of hunters hoping to capture it. These peoples believed in a magical connection between such ceremonies and the forces of nature. They believed that drama would grant them success in meeting their real needs.

Imagine yourself gathering at night with fellow hunters. See the campfire casting eerie shadows in the smoke. A drum beats steadily as members of the hunting party dance in a circle. Then the chosen player puts on the antlers of a deer caught long ago. In so doing, he *becomes* the deer soon to be captured. The other hunters circle in to "kill" the "deer" with their spears. Tomorrow's hunt is assured success through this ritual.

Teaching Ceremony

As more formal religions developed, drama continued to have a religious purpose. In fact, the first actual "theaters" were sacred spaces. Since most people were not able to read, religious "plays" were performed to teach important beliefs. For example, the crowning of the Pharaoh in Ancient Egypt was accompanied by plays that taught about his divine birth. Following the Pharaoh's death, additional plays were performed above his tomb to celebrate the Pharaoh's rebirth.

Ancient Festival

Before the "official" beginnings of Western drama in classical Athens, the early Greeks made use of choral hymns and dances in their worship. During seasonal fertility rites, they shared in lively festivities. Performers pretended to be birds and other animals by wearing masks and costumes. The classical forms of both tragedy and comedy are said to have sprung from these folk celebrations.

You may not recognize it, but today's drama is actually the direct descendant of primitive ritual, teaching ceremony, and ancient festival. By communicating powerful emotions and ideas, modern drama, too, has the power to transform, educate, and entertain its audiences.

Like primitive rituals, contemporary drama depends on our ability to imagine. The instinct for drama seems to be rooted deeply in human beings of all cultures.

Children are born "actors"—they love to pretend. And even adult playgoers today willingly suspend their realistic thought processes when the auditorium lights go down and the curtain goes up. One part of us knows that what we see is all make-believe. Yet, another part of us eagerly participates in the illusion created by scenery, stage lighting, costumes, makeup, and, most of all, skillful actors telling a really good story.

*Drama: A Comprehensive Guide
to Dramatic Elements and Style*

Name _____ Date _____

 *Exercise 1.3*

Ritual and Real Life

The dramatic rituals of early peoples had important connections to their daily lives. Are there things in your life that could also be described as "ritual"—even if not "dramatic ritual"?

Directions: On the lines below, list things that have a ritual quality for you as an individual and for your culture as a whole. Write each item as if you were trying to explain it to someone unfamiliar with these rituals.

Example	**Ritual:** Every day in school the entire group stands and faces a rectangular cloth, which symbolizes our country. We chant in unison a promise of loyalty to the symbol and to the country.

Ritual: _____

_____

_____

Ritual: _____

_____

_____

Ritual: _____

_____

_____

Ritual: _____

_____

_____

Ritual: _____

_____

_____

Ritual: _____

_____

_____

Drama: A Comprehensive Guide
to Dramatic Elements and Style

Name _____   Date _____

 Exercise 1.4

Compare Today's Rock Concert with Primitive Ritual

Directions

A. Try to imagine what it must have been like to be part of a primitive ritual ceremony, including elements such as music, dancing, costumes, and masks. In the space below, describe the scene you imagined:

_____

_____

_____

_____

_____

B. Now—either from your own experience or from your imagination—describe the sights and sounds of a rock concert:

_____

_____

_____

_____

_____

C. In what ways are the experiences similar? How are they different? How are both related to your definition of "drama"?

_____

_____

_____

_____

_____

_____

_____

Drama: A Comprehensive Guide
to Dramatic Elements and Style

Name _____   Date _____

A Short History of Western Drama

When you watch a live stage play, film, or TV program, you probably never stop to think that the drama you are watching is built on traditions that are up to 2,500 years old. Yet it's true. The dramatic conventions that we take for granted today have been evolving from many different cultures for 25 centuries.

The Beginnings of Tragic Drama

As a citizen of Athens in the fifth century B.C., each year you would have attended all-day drama competitions. These play contests were staged at the huge **amphitheater** built into the side of the hillside in the shadow of the temple to Athena on the Acropolis.

This vast outdoor theater seated up to 20,000 spectators. They sat on tiers of stone benches somewhat like the seating you would find today in a large football stadium. The acoustics in this theater—as in many such theaters throughout classical Greece—were amazingly accurate. Even a stage whisper could easily be heard by spectators in the very last row.

In the earliest form of Greek drama, the actors performed on a bare circular acting and dancing space called the **orchestra**. There was no scenery at all. Later on, a structure of columns with three entrance ways—called the **skene**—was added behind the orchestra space.

All the character parts in a play were performed by only two or three actors. In Aeschylus's play *Agamemnon*, there are six roles: the King, the King's Cousin, the Queen, the Captive, the Herald, and the Watchman. All the roles, male and female, were played by just two male actors.

In order to portray individual characters in the drama, the actors wore different robes and large masks. In addition to representing specific characters, each mask was constructed so that the mouthpiece amplified the actor's voice.

In addition to the individualized central characters, a **chorus** of masked actors spoke as a group. The chorus spoke their lines in poetic rhythms, commenting on the action of the play. Since we know that music also accompanied performances, it is believed that the chorus moved in dancelike motions to fit the rhythms of their speeches. The speeches spoken by the chorus often commented on the actions of the main characters. The playwright also used these speeches to give the audience descriptions of the setting and background plot information.

The high point of Greek tragic drama is attributed to three great playwrights: **Aeschylus,** known for his trilogy of plays called the *Oresteia* (*Agamemnon, The Libation Bearers,* and *The Eumenides*); **Sophocles** (496?–406 B.C.), author of the trilogy of Oedipus plays (*Oedipus The King, Oedipus at Colonus,* and *Antigone*); and **Euripides** (480?–406? B.C.), author of tragedies such as *Medea, Alcestis,* and *Hippolytus.*

Rather than presenting original plots, these tragic plays were based on myths and legends that the audience already knew. The audience knew in advance how each play would end. This meant they could concentrate on appreciating the poetry of the speeches, the skill of the actor's presentations, and the spectacle of the masks, costumes, and movements of the chorus.

(continued)

Drama: A Comprehensive Guide to Dramatic Elements and Style

Name _____   Date _____

Exercise 1.5

Stage a Scene from Greek Tragedy

Theater historians are not absolutely sure how Greek tragedy was performed originally. When modern directors stage one of the great classical tragedies, they must decide how to stage it for modern audiences.

Directions: Working in small groups, choose a single scene from a contemporary translation of a drama by Aeschylus, Sophocles, or Euripedes—preferably one that involves both main characters and chorus.

Each group should start by discussing questions regarding how to stage the scene. Such questions might include:

1. Which group members will play the main characters? Which group members will make

   up the chorus? _____

   _____

2. Will your production attempt to create masks and/or costumes? If so, will they try to imitate original Greek masks and costumes? Or will the scene be staged in modern dress?

   _____

   _____

3. Will the lines of the chorus always be spoken by the entire chorus? Or will lines be broken up in combinations—some to be recited by all, some by one chorus member, some by another?

   _____

   _____

4. Will the chorus move or make gestures when they speak?

   _____

   _____

   _____

Greek play in masks, National Theater

To prepare for making these—and other—decisions, groups may decide to do more research about what is known about the original staging of Greek tragic drama.

After each of the scenes has been performed, join in a general discussion about the challenges you faced in "interpreting" these classic scripts.

*Drama: A Comprehensive Guide
to Dramatic Elements and Style*

Name _____ Date _____

A Short History of Western Drama *(continued)*

The Beginnings of Comedy

The ancient Greeks also gave us the foundations of comedy. At first, comic plays were performed immediately following the more serious tragic plays. They used some of the same theatrical elements, such as the chorus, but in new ways.

The first comic playwright, **Aristophanes** (448?–385? B.C.), used the chorus to comment on social and political problems. Also, instead of using plots based on traditional myths, he made up his own original plots.

Aristophanes' comic plots were written to satirize political and social issues of his day.

Example	His play *The Birds* poked fun at the teachings of the philosopher Socrates.

The later Greek comic playwright **Menander** (342–291? B.C.) originated a new style of comedy. His plays were known for comic character types and complicated plot situations. Only one of Menander's plays exists complete today. However, we know that his work greatly influenced the work of two later Roman comic playwrights, **Plautus** (254?–184 B.C.) and **Terence** (185?–159? B.C.). They reworked the material from Menander's plays for their own purposes.

Example	Plautus's *Mostelleria* (*The Haunted House*) includes intricate plot, fast pace, mistaken identities, and humorous character types.

As a modern viewer, you are heir to the traditions of ancient comedy every time you turn on your favorite television situation comedy. A more direct way to sample Roman comedy is by watching *A Funny Thing Happened on the Way to the Forum*. The authors of this musical comedy combined characters and situations from all 21 of Plautus's existing plays.

(continued)

Name _____   Date _____

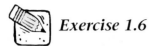 **Exercise 1.6**

Ancient Comedy at Work Today

The comedies of the Greeks and Romans often included some stock concepts:

- comic character types, such as "the scheming servant"
- complicated plot situations

- mistaken identities
- characters who show up at inconvenient times

Directions: Think about comedies you have seen, both plays and movies. Name at least three comedies, and list the comic elements they share with ancient Greek and Roman comedies.

Example	**Comedy:** Shakespeare's *The Comedy of Errors* **Comic Elements:** mistaken identity—two sets of twins, separated at birth, end up in Syracuse. Confusion ensues when the pair from Ephesus are mistaken for the twins from Syracuse. The plot is taken from Plautus's *Menaechmi*.

Comedy: _____

Comic Elements:_____

_____

Comedy: _____

Comic Elements:_____

_____

Comedy: _____

Comic Elements:_____

_____

Name _____   Date _____

A Short History of Western Drama *(continued)*

New Forms of Drama in the Middle Ages

After the decline of the Roman Empire, drama in Europe was dormant for nearly a thousand years. Eventually, during the Middle Ages, new theatrical forms began to emerge. This new drama was connected to the Christian Church, which was central to everyday life in Europe.

At first, short religious plays were included within church services. They were performed like the services themselves—in Latin. Since few churchgoers understood Latin, however, the plays began to be performed in the language of the people. Eventually, these plays were moved outside the church altogether. They gave rise to cycles of **Mystery Plays** that told stories from the Bible in dramatic form.

The Wakefield Cycle

In certain towns, such as Wakefield, England (c.1385), these Mystery Play cycles were produced annually. Different trade guilds—such as the carpenters or metalworkers—would take on producing one of the plays. Some of the individual plays were very serious, while others included a great deal of broad humor.

Example	*The Second Shepherds' Play* interweaves the actions of comic shepherds with the solemn birth of the Christ child.

A complete Mystery cycle could include as many as 48 plays. In some locations, they were performed over a period of days. These plays were performed from pageant wagons which would move through the town. Guild members performed their individual play a number of times during the day, moving their wagon from station to station. Spectators needed only to stand in one spot to observe each play of the cycle performed in sequence.

Elsewhere, these plays were performed on fixed stages. This encouraged the development of scenery and special effects. It also led to the introduction of a director to organize the whole production.

Morality Plays

Another type of drama evolved in the Middle Ages called the **Morality Play**. Morality plays were also acted by trade guilds, but individually, rather than in cycles. They used the dramatic form of **allegory** to teach spiritual lessons. In an allegory, each character is a symbol for something. The way the characters interact expresses something about human existence.

Example	*Everyman* (1485)—Everyman receives a summons from Death; tries to escape, accompanied only by Good Deeds; finally accepts his fate.

(continued)

Drama: A Comprehensive Guide to Dramatic Elements and Style

Name _____   Date _____

A Short History of Western Drama *(continued)*

Italy's Street Theater— **Commedia dell'arte**

Beginning in the sixteenth century in Renaissance Italy, another form of drama was born. The **commedia dell'arte** was the roving street theater of the day. ("Dell'arte" in Italian means "skilled" or "professional.")

A *commedia dell'arte* company consisted of 10 to 12 professional actors. They were skilled at pantomime, acrobatics, physical humor, and creating humorous character voices. These troupes included women as well as men.

The *commedia dell'arte* troupes came into being at a time when other Renaissance playwrights were rediscovering the classical comedies of Menander, Plautus, and Terence. Yet this particular form of comic drama had no set dialogue. The players worked from outlines of plots. For each performance, the dialogue was **improvised**—made up on the spot.

Each actor played the part of a stock character that was well known to the audience.

Example	Pantalone—lecherous old man
	The Captain—boastful soldier
	The Doctor—show-off who uses big words

Each actor wore a costume designed to allow audiences to easily identify the character he or she was playing. Certain characters also wore comic half-masks with exaggerated noses and cheeks. These masks covered only the upper half of their faces to allow the actor's voice to be heard.

| **Example** | Pantalone—costume included tight red vest, red breeches and stockings, soft slippers, long black coat, soft cap, brown mask with large hooked nose, straggling grey beard |

A few of the plots of the commedia dell'arte were serious, but most were comic. They revolved around love and intrigue, disguises, and people at cross-purposes.

In many ways, these Italian comedians were like modern improvisational comedy groups . These groups make up humorous characters and skits from suggestions from the audience.

(continued)

Drama: A Comprehensive Guide to Dramatic Elements and Style

Name _____ Date _____

A Short History of Western Drama *(continued)*

Drama in Elizabethan England

The late sixteenth and early seventeenth century was a period of greatness in the English theater.

Christopher Marlowe

Christopher Marlowe (1564–93) was a colorful figure who was murdered mysteriously before his thirtieth birthday. He is considered the greatest early Elizabethan playwright. Marlowe's most respected play, *Doctor Faustus*, tells the story of a man who sells his soul to the devil for forbidden knowledge and power.

Marlowe's dramatic language was full of images drawn from his extensive knowledge and interests. He was the first English dramatist to write dialogue in blank verse—unrhymed poetic lines. Marlowe's plays served as models for a playwright born in the same year, William Shakespeare.

William Shakespeare

A man of far-ranging talents, **William Shakespeare** (1564–1616) knew the theater from inside out. Not only was he the author of over 40 plays, he also was an actor and manager of his own theater company.

William Shakespeare

Perhaps never in the history of drama has a playwright produced so many truly great plays. Shakespeare was the master of all dramatic forms—tragedies (such as *Romeo and Juliet, Macbeth, Othello,* and *Hamlet*), comedies (such as *A Midsummer Night's Dream, As You Like It,* and *The Taming of the Shrew*), histories (such as *Henry IV, Part 1* and *Henry V*), and tragicomedies (such as *The Tempest*).

Shakespeare's dramas continue to be produced for stage, film, and television 350 years after he wrote them. They are also used as the basis for new plays and movies.

| **Example** | *West Side Story*—musical based on *Romeo and Juliet* |

In Shakespeare's own day, boys played all the women's parts. Today, actresses love to play Shakespeare's women because of his deep insight into the psychology of women.

The Elizabethan Stage

The Elizabethan performing space had a great effect on the dramas of the day. The Globe Theater—where many of Shakespeare's plays were performed—opened in 1599. The Globe was built in the shape of a hexagon around an open-air inner court. More than 1500 people could attend a single performance. The lowest-paying audience members stood in the open courtyard—also referred to as "the pit." The more expensive seats were in one of three semicircular galleries. Plays took place in the afternoon.

The layout of the theater provided a variety of spaces for different scenes. On the ground level, a forestage jutted out into the audience; "outdoor" scenes were played on it. Behind this was a curtained inner stage for "interior" scenes. There was also an upper level with another curtained inner stage and a balcony.

Because there was no main curtain or scenery to be changed, the action of Shakespeare's plays was continuous. The bare playing space required the dramatist to create a sense of time and place entirely with words. Without question, Shakespeare proved himself to be up to the challenge.

(continued)

Drama: A Comprehensive Guide to Dramatic Elements and Style

Name _____   Date _____

A Short History of Western Drama *(continued)*

French Theater in the Seventeenth Century

Until the early years of the seventeenth century, French drama consisted of small troupes of players. The comedies they performed were based on commedia dell' arte, with stock characters and costumes. Then, around 1625, a new era in French theater began.

Pierre Corneille

Pierre Corneille (1606–84) studied to be a lawyer, but he enjoyed watching plays. In 1629 he wrote a comedy, *Mélite*. It was different from the farces of most French comedies. Instead of comic servants, it focused on the misunderstandings of two lovers. Other playwrights soon adopted this approach. A new style of French comedy was born.

Corneille also changed French tragedy with his play *Le Cid*. The theme of this play is love versus honor. The hero, Roderigue, and the heroine, Chimène, must choose between their love for each other and their duty to their parents. *Le Cid* was a huge success, but some critics attacked it. The controversy resulted in a new focus on neoclassical themes in French drama.

Jean Racine

Classical French tragedy reached its peak in the work of **Jean Racine** (1639–99). Many earlier plays involved complex plots and one-dimensional characters. In Racine's plays, the plots are very simple. The charac-

ters are complex, torn between desire and duty. The action of the play consists of the main character's internal conflict. Racine's masterpiece, *Phèdre*, was his last play as a professional playwright.

Molière's "Comedy of Manners"

Yet another genre of comedy, known as the "comedy of manners," was perfected in seventeenth-century France by a theater manager and playwright called by a name he made up for himself, **Molière** (1622–73).

Molière had a keen eye for satirizing the pretensions and human weaknesses of the Parisian society of the time. His plays still speak to today's audiences.

Example	*The Bourgeois Gentleman* satirized social ambition with the story of a rich man who wants to join the upper class

Translations of his most popular plays (such as *The Miser*, *Tartuffe*, *The Bourgeois Gentleman*, and *The Imaginary Invalid*) are performed by theater companies around the world.

In these and other plays, Molière holds a mirror up to the weaknesses of pride, vanity, and selfishness that make us all too human. Because Molière knew human nature so well, his plays, like Shakespeare's, have a timeless quality. They ring true to theatergoers far beyond the original audience of his time.

(continued)

Drama: A Comprehensive Guide to Dramatic Elements and Style

Name _____ Date _____

A Short History of Western Drama *(continued)*

The Emergence of Modern Drama

Theater historians tend to agree that the true beginnings of modern drama can be seen in the work of three theatrical giants. The history of twentieth-century drama was founded on their theatrical innovations.

Henrik Ibsen

The nineteenth century had seen the development of well-crafted, three-act dramas. Norwegian playwright **Henrik Ibsen** (1828–1906) took the concept of the "well-made play" and added a greater realism and psychological depth. The sets for his plays were highly realistic. And his theatrical language mixed realistic dialogue with poetic concentration and symbolism. In his most respected plays (such as *A Doll's House, The Wild Duck,* and *Hedda Gabler*), Ibsen shocked audiences by his courage to openly speak about serious issues of his day.

Example	In *A Doll's House* Nora realizes that she has always been treated as a doll. She decides to leave her husband to become a person in her own right.

August Strindberg

August Strindberg (1849–1912) of Sweden added to the passion for realism and truth-telling begun by Ibsen. Strindberg's penetrating insight into exaggerated psychological states led him to invent new "surreal" (dreamlike) dramatic forms in such plays as *Miss Julie* and *The Ghost Sonata.* His theatrical "experiments" greatly influenced the dramatic range of playwrights that followed him.

Anton Chekhov

The Russian playwright **Anton Chekhov** (1860–1904) might be considered the most original of these dramatists. Chekhov's characters are neither heroes or villains. They are caught in situations where they cannot make significant changes in their lives. In Chekhov's plays, tragedy is not the result of a clash between individuals. It is the wearing away of life in ordinary people. As a result, Chekhov's drama emphasizes character and atmosphere over plot and action. His plays have been called "tragi-comedy" because they are both sad and humorous at the same time.

Example	In *The Sea Gull* Trepler, a poet, tries to create new dramatic forms, but fails. He comes to realize that it's important to write, whether or not the form is new. Still, this is not enough for him. When he loses his love for a second time, he shoots himself.

(continued)

Drama: A Comprehensive Guide to Dramatic Elements and Style

Name _____   Date _____

A Short History of Western Drama *(continued)*

Giants of Twentieth-Century Drama

The twentieth century was a time of continuing experiments in dramatic forms. A few names and their contributions might suggest some of the different paths that drama has taken in the past 100 years.

Luigi Pirandello

Italian playwright **Luigi Pirandello** (1867–1936) asks questions explored in many ways by other twentieth-century playwrights: What is the nature of a character's real self? What is the difference between illusion and reality?

Example	In *Six Characters in Search of an Author*, a writer did not finish a story. The characters he created insist on playing out their lives, and invade the rehearsal of another play.

George Bernard Shaw

The Irish playwright, **George Bernard Shaw** (1856–1950), developed a concept of drama as a "theater of ideas." His plays, such as *Saint Joan, Pygmalion* (on which the musical *My Fair Lady* is based), and *Man and Superman*, used realistic stage plots that were full of clever dialogue between articulate characters to explore social problems of his—and our—day.

Example	In *Arms and the Man*, Shaw exploded the "romance" of war. Characters include a soldier who carries chocolates instead of bullets, because chocolate is more likely to be useful, and the war hero whose charge would have been fatal if the enemy hadn't had the wrong ammunition.

Bertolt Brecht

To a similar purpose, the German dramatist **Bertolt Brecht** (1898–1956), in plays such as *Mother Courage and Her Children* and *The Good Woman of Setzuan*, developed a sprawling "non-dramatic" style of theater designed to educate audiences about political themes. His plays use many devices, such as signs that drop down to comment on each scene and specialized acting styles, to continually remind audiences that what they are watching is not "real."

Eugene O'Neill

American playwright **Eugene O'Neill** (1888–1953) brought a new maturity to American drama. Still considered one of America's greatest playwrights, he was deeply influenced by the groundbreaking contributions of Ibsen and Strindberg. His plays, such as *The Iceman Cometh* and *A Long Day's Journey into Night,* show deep insight into the psychological and social forces that drive characters to act in the way they do.

(continued)

Name _____   Date _____

A Short History of Western Drama *(continued)*

Eugene Ionesco and Samuel Beckett

Playwrights **Eugene Ionesco** (1912–94) and **Samuel Beckett** (1906–89) developed what has been called the "theater of the absurd." Building on the earlier surrealist drama of playwrights such as Strindberg, famous plays like Ionesco's *Rhinoceros* and Beckett's *Waiting for Godot* present non-realistic characters in dreamlike situations designed to explore the interior landscapes of our innermost hopes and fears.

Dario Fo

Italian playwright **Dario Fo** uses a variety of dramatic forms to comment on society. His provocative plays make use of the commedia dell'arte tradition of stock characters, slapstick, masks, and double roles. To this he adds real names and places to expose exploitation. These techniques let him use such plays as *Accidental Death of an Anarchist* and *Can't Pay? Won't Pay!* as a political weapon.

Endgame **by Samuel Beckett**

*Drama: A Comprehensive Guide
to Dramatic Elements and Style*

Name _____   Date _____

 Exercise 1.7

An Illustrated Timeline of Western Drama

One of the best ways to understand the path of development from the Greeks to modern drama is through seeing illustrations from each of the eras and cultures involved.

Directions: Begin collecting materials to create a timeline that illustrates the history of Western drama, primarily in pictures.

From library books, textbooks, magazine articles, Internet pages, and other sources, collect illustrations to show what the actors, dramatists, dramas, and performing spaces of each era looked like. (You may bring in the original source or make photocopies of specific illustrations and photographs.)

When all the materials have been collected, arrange them in chronological order to construct your illustrated timeline of drama history.

Lysistrata—**Royal Shakespeare Company—visiting Greek company**

*Drama: A Comprehensive Guide
to Dramatic Elements and Style*

Name _____   Date _____

Styles of Drama in Other Cultures

The dramatic traditions of other cultures, such as those of India, China, and Japan, developed styles that are strikingly different from those of our Western culture. Unlike Western drama, many non-Western performance styles do not emphasize the presentation of realistic characters or plots. In the development of modern theater, especially in the twentieth century, Western playwrights have borrowed from Eastern theatrical techniques.

The Dramatic Arts of India

The dramatic tradition in India is one of the world's oldest. According to legend, many centuries ago, the people of India had become addicted to pleasure. The god Indra approached Brahma, the Creator of the Universe, and asked him for an entertainment that all people could enjoy. Brahma agreed, and created the art of Sanskrit drama.

**Chau Dancers in masks—
visiting company from India**

Sanskrit drama was at its height about the fifth century A.D. It took much of its material from two Hindu epics, the *Mahabharata* and the *Ramayana*. Since the aim of the drama was to create harmony, all plays ended happily. Right and wrong were clearly differentiated. The story often included several subplots, some serious, some farcical. Even the dialogue was often complex. In very emotional scenes, verse might be used. In more ordinary scenes, the characters might speak prose. Some dialogue might be in Sanskrit, the language spoken by educated people. Some might be in Prakrit, the everyday dialect.

In one popular kind of play, heroic drama, an ideal hero defends a just cause. These plays often include a love story where an evil force keeps the lovers apart until the end of the play.

Example	In the play *Shakuntala*, by Kalidasa, King Dushyanta is the ideal hero. He falls in love with Shakuntala, the foster daughter of a hermit. A rejected suitor curses the lovers, and they are separated. Finally, at the end of the play, they are reunited.

In Sanskrit plays, no scenery was used. The actors used stylized movement to show where and when a scene took place.

Example	A walk around the stage indicated a long journey.

(continued)

*Drama: A Comprehensive Guide
to Dramatic Elements and Style*

Name _____   Date _____

Styles of Drama in Other Cultures *(continued)*

The actors were only allowed to use certain movements and gestures, all of which had a precise meaning. These movements could be combined to create a complex sign language. The actors' costumes and makeup were also used to convey information. This included the character's social position, caste (social class), place of birth, even historical period.

Example	Red stood for high caste, and blue stood for low caste.

The Sanskrit theater came to an end around the twelfth century, but its traditions were kept alive in folk plays and puppet plays. During the British occupation of India, Western-style drama was introduced. In the twentieth century playwrights like Ramashankar Roy (1860–1910) and Rabindranath Tagore (1861–1941) wrote plays that blended Indian and Western traditions.

However, Indian theater is still heavily influenced by classical forms. By the 1960s, many writers overcame the barrier of regional languages to produce good works for a national audience. These plays combined styles and techniques from different traditions: Sanskrit theater, folk theater, and Western theater.

Example	Vijay Tendulkar's 1972 play *Ghashiram Kotwal* used traditional folk forms in modern contemporary theater.

(continued)

Name _____   Date _____

Styles of Drama in Other Cultures *(continued)*

The Dramatic Arts of China

Traditional Chinese theater combines everyday language with music and song. The drama deals with characters familiar to the audience and with themes about practical real-life issues. Thus, the Chinese opera, as the Chinese drama is called, has always been very popular with the common people.

Chinese drama emphasizes music rather than dance. The orchestra plays an important role in the action, somewhat like the soundtrack of a film today. Music sets the tempo for characters' exits and entrances. It also heightens the effect of dramatic scenes.

The actors, too, are first and foremost singers. They also have skills as acrobats and mimes. Their stage movements are precisely coordinated with their vocal rhythms. In fact, the entire performance is conducted by an orchestra leader, whose drum and clappers provide the rhythm for the musicians and actors.

The Chinese Stage

Chinese drama has no scenery. The square stage projects into the auditorium and is bare, except for a carpet. There is no front curtain, but the stage is curtained at the sides and back. All entrances are made from the right side of the stage and exits are made to the left.

Stage props are simple, but used very imaginatively. An ordinary wooden table and two straight chairs are all that is used to enact scenes such as storms and battles.

Example	chair on table—mountain to be climbed
	a cloth between the chairs—a bed

Black flags stand for a high wind, while flags with waves on them suggest water. A horse is symbolized by a whip in the actor's hand. An actor carrying an oar is imagined to be in a boat.

To suggest a change of scene, the actors simply walk around in a circle. To suggest an army entering a city, a few actors carrying large banners march beneath a painted arch held up by property men. Because property men are dressed in black, they are presumed to be "invisible" to the audience. However, they are active on stage throughout the performance.

The Actor's Training

In Chinese drama, the actor's training is very important. Actors are trained to manipulate their voices to fit a range of serious or comic roles. They are also trained in mime, such as learning how to pretend to fight with swords or to row a boat. They must also learn a repertoire of highly stylized gestures. The wave of a finger, for instance, can suggest very specific meanings.

The Chinese opera has four main roles: the male; the female; the "painted face" (which represents aggressive male characters such as warriors, bandits, etc.); and the clown. No attempt is made to give these characters individual personalities.

(continued)

Name _____   Date _____

Styles of Drama in Other Cultures *(continued)*

Chinese opera actor in full costume backstage

Gorgeous costumes and striking makeup indicate the identity of each character.

Example	outlaw chief—dark blue face, scarlet eyebrows and beard, extra pair of eyes painted on cheeks

A Chinese opera performance is very long, made up of many episodes. Yet, with a nearly bare stage and few props, a world of unlimited imagination can be created.

The Dramatic Arts of Japan

The traditional drama of Japan includes four separate performing traditions: **Bugaku** dance theater; classic **Noh** drama and comic **Kyogen** plays; **Bunraku** puppet theater; and the popular **Kabuki** theater.

Bugaku

Bugaku theater relies heavily on dance. The movements of the dancers are slow and graceful as they act out portions of an old tale or a dance of celebration. All the performers are men.

The dancing is accompanied by *gagaku*, music by wind, stringed, and percussion instruments.

A bugaku performance is very ritualistic. The musicians file on, followed by the dancers. Like the music, the traditional dance patterns use body movements that are unfamiliar to Western spectators. Elaborate movements often mirror each other. They are performed by a single dancer or sometimes by pairs of dancers.

The stage is very colorful, with a green cloth covering and red varnished railings with gold decoration. The audience sits or stands on three sides of the stage. The costumes are also very decorative, including many varieties of masks and helmets.

Noh

Noh drama is considered the classical theater of Japan. In many ways, it shares qualities of ancient Greek drama including the use of masks, a chorus, formal dance, and dignified poetry.

Over 1000 years old, Noh drama was intended only for a small group of nobles at the Japanese court. Even when performed today, performances are very slow. Long intervals pass onstage without motion. Performances are full of obscure body movements. They are chanted in an ancient poetic language that is difficult for most Japanese audiences to understand.

(continued)

Drama: A Comprehensive Guide to Dramatic Elements and Style

Name _____ Date _____

Styles of Drama in Other Cultures *(continued)*

A Noh performance does not look or sound like real life. Its stories are simple and there is no dramatic conflict. If the play requires a boat or a hut, these are represented by a skeletal frame that only suggests their shape. Depending on how it is held, a folding fan may represent a variety of objects. It can stand for a sword, a letter, the rising moon, or falling rain.

**Japanese traditional theater,
Edinburgh Festival, Scotland**

Noh plays are usually performed on an 18-foot-square bare stage . A narrow runway leads to the stage from the dressing room. Performances are accompanied by drums, a high-pitched flute, and chanting by a chorus of six or eight men.

The orchestra and singers play an important part in the performance. Sometimes there is a stark contrast between what is seen (for instance, a character approaching in slow motion) and what is heard (the music of the orchestra and singers suggesting great speed).

Noh actors must train from childhood to master the complex gestures of Noh drama. All parts, including female roles, are played by men and boys. In any scene, there are only two important roles: the principal character and the subordinate character. Each character wears elegant embroidered costumes patterned on medieval court dress. The principal character usually wears a painted mask carved from wood.

Today, a traditional Noh program consists of three serious plays, with two humorous shorter **Kyogen** plays performed in between. In contrast to the serious and slow-moving Noh plays, the comical Kyogen plays are shorter and much livelier. Using simple props and mime techniques, these Kyogen plays deal with universal comic situations such as servants outwitting their masters. Since the Kyogen plays are much more accessible to modern audiences, they are often now also performed alone.

Bunraku

Bunraku is the puppet theater of Japan. It combines manipulation of life-like puppets with the singing of a narrator and musical accompaniment.

Each puppet is about half life-size and is handled by a team of three puppeteers. By means of strings inside the puppet's head, the chief puppeteer controls the movable mouth, eyebrows, and eyelids, as well as the right arm and hand of the puppet. Assistants control the rest of the puppet. The movements of the puppets are remarkably graceful and lifelike.

(continued)

*Drama: A Comprehensive Guide
to Dramatic Elements and Style*

Name _____ Date _____

Styles of Drama in Other Cultures *(continued)*

Bunraku puppet operators are completely visible to the audience throughout the play.

The puppeteers never speak. Instead, a narrator-singer sits on a rostrum projecting from the stage. He chants the narration of the story as well as the spoken words of each character. This is so demanding on the narrator-singer's voice that it often requires a change of narrators during a performance. The narrator-singer is also accompanied by music provided by the samisen, a three-stringed, plucked instrument.

Unlike Noh theater, the Bunraku stage uses elaborate scenery and various techniques and devices for changing scenes rapidly. The precise teamwork required between the puppet operators, musician, and narrator requires many years of training.

Kabuki

In contrast to the aristocratic Noh drama, Kabuki theater is the theater of the common people of Japan. In many ways, it is a blend of the Japanese performing arts. A single performance can include a dance based on a Noh play or a Kyogen, part of a Bunraku performance, and acts from plays written especially for the Kabuki.

Although the plays are set in realistic scenery, Kabuki plots are not drawn from real life. Unlike Noh drama, serious and comic content are often mixed in the same scene. Kabuki theater is full of visual effects. Warriors dance in huge battle scenes. Elaborate settings change on a revolving stage floor. Scenery and actors on elevators appear and disappear in full view of the audience. In some Kabuki plays, the actors wear white, red, and black makeup to symbolize power and strength. Costumes may weigh as much as fifty pounds.

Women played all Kabuki parts until a ban in 1680. From that point on, male actors have played both male and female roles. Kabuki performances require highly skilled actors, trained from childhood in dance, voice, and acrobatics. Kabuki actors can play a wide range of human characters. They can also play a wide variety of non-human parts, including animals such as horses, foxes, and dogs.

Kabuki Theater

*Drama: A Comprehensive Guide
to Dramatic Elements and Style*

Name _____   Date _____

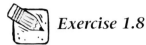 *Exercise 1.8*

"Reviewing" a Non-Western Drama Performance

This assignment invites you to learn more about one of the performance topics introduced in the reading—and then to write an imaginary theater review telling about what it would be like to actually attend a performance.

Directions: First, choose *one* of the non-Western performance modes below:

* Hindu drama

* Chinese Opera

* Japanese Bugaku

* Japanese Noh drama

* Japanese Kyogen plays

* Japanese Bunraku puppet theater

* Japanese Kabuki theater

Consult library resources (books and periodicals) as well as Internet sites to learn more about the area you have chosen to research.

When you have completed your research, write an imaginary theater review of what it would be like to attend a performance of the genre you chose. Include as many specifics as you can. Use these questions as a guideline.

1. What would you *see*? (Describe the stage, scenery, costumes, makeup, props, the actor's movements and gestures, etc.)

2. What would you *hear*? (Describe the music, instruments used, singing, actor's use of voice, etc.)

3. How would you probably *react* as a Western audience member?

Drama: A Comprehensive Guide to Dramatic Elements and Style

Name _____   Date _____

Exercise 1.9

Make a Bunraku Puppet

The Bunraku puppets of Japan are over half life-size and are operated by three puppeteers simultaneously.

Directions: As a class, research more about the mechanics and operation of the actual Japanese Bunraku puppets.

Then, form into puppeteer teams of three students each. Using what you have learned about Bunraku puppets as a guide, each team will create a three-person puppet. The puppet does not have to copy the Bunraku *exactly*—but it does have to require three persons to operate it.

When all teams have created puppets, show off your puppet in a brief performance for the rest of the class.

If students are interested, members of your class could write a play to include all the puppets—and puppeteers—to be performed for other classes in your school.

Samisen player, traditional accompaniment to Bunraku puppet theater

Drama: A Comprehensive Guide
to Dramatic Elements and Style

Name _____   Date _____

The Power of Live Theater

Audiences today experience drama in a variety of media—stage, screen, and television. However, there are important differences between experiencing a *live* dramatic performance and a film or television show.

The Effect of the Audience

Whenever drama is experienced in the company of an audience, it becomes a shared experience. The audience is an important part of the dramatic event.

Even when you are watching a film in a movie theater or a TV program at home, your reactions are heightened and even changed by the reactions of others around you. When drama is performed live in front of an audience, the shared theater experience becomes even more powerful. One important reason is that film and television performances are "frozen." The actors on the screen are not affected by the reactions of those who are watching, no matter how strongly viewers may be reacting to their performances. During a live theater performance, there is a direct communication between the audience and the performers. This is unlike any other "fixed" dramatic medium.

Did you ever stop to think that, because theater is live, no two performances are ever *exactly* alike? Even when a play's script and staging stays the same from performance to performance, the unique reactions of each individual audience can affect how the actors perform. It also affects how other audience members react at that performance.

Think about the moment *in Romeo and Juliet* when Romeo attempts to stop the sword fight between Juliet's cousin, Tybalt, and his own best friend, Mercutio. By trying to separate them, Romeo ends up being the cause of Tybalt's killing Mercutio. It is a dramatic moment. Some audiences gasp, others cry, and others do not react at all.

Events in Real Time

A second important difference is that the stage performances happen in "real time" for both the actors and the audience. Most often, film and pre-recorded TV programs have been edited. The actors' performances have been constructed by piecing together pieces of scenes. These have often been photographed out of sequence. Many times, film actors are required to act bits of the same scene over and over from different camera angles.

Sir Ian McKellan as Romeo

(continued)

Drama: A Comprehensive Guide to Dramatic Elements and Style

Name _____ Date _____

The Power of Live Theater *(continued)*

In contrast, a live dramatic play is performed continuously in front of the audience. Scene follows scene in sequence. The action "happens" to the actors at the same time that it "happens" in front of the audience. This allows the actor to fully rediscover his or her character in each performance. In this way, the actor can be more identified with the moment-by-moment experience of the character—which the audience feels, too.

Think about the actors who play the characters of Helen Keller and her teacher, Annie Sullivan, in William Gibson's play *The Miracle Worker.* In every performance, these characters must work through the same dramatic struggles that reach the final moments when Helen comes to speak her first word. Seeing performers acting out this relationship *live* in front of you adds an extra dimension to the drama.

Viewing Point

A third difference is that with film and television, the camera controls the viewer's point of view. Even when you are viewing a live TV show, the director determines from which camera you will see the action. At a live performance, however, spectators are free to look at any part of the stage at any time. They can choose for themselves just how and where they want to view the action.

Think about what it's like to watch a large dance number in a musical play such as *West Side Story.* Or consider a play with many characters in colorful costumes and makeup such as *Cats.* Much of the excitement comes from the fact that there is so much going on—at the same time!

The Bread and Puppet Theater

*Drama: A Comprehensive Guide
to Dramatic Elements and Style*

Name _____   Date _____

 Exercise 1.10

Two Live Theater Experiments

To appreciate the unique audience-to-performer communication at work in a live theater performance, try these two experiments in your classroom.

Directions

1. First, volunteer (as a "performer") to stand in front of your class to recite from memory a nursery rhyme that you know well (e.g. "Mary Had A Little Lamb" or "Twinkle, Twinkle, Little Star").

With the class as "audience," instruct the other students to allow you to get started on your recitation without interruption. However, once you have begun, instruct them to start to "heckle" you by making faces, distracting sounds, etc.

This exercise will provide immediate proof of the power of a live audience to have an impact on a live performer's performance!

2. To provide a direct contrast with this first experiment, your teacher will bring a television (or radio) into the classroom.

Turn on any program broadcast. Then, invite the class to heckle it! You can also change channels randomly while the heckling continues.

No matter how disruptively the class behaves, these performances—even if they are "live" on the air—will not be affected at all!

*Drama: A Comprehensive Guide
to Dramatic Elements and Style*

Name _____   Date _____

 Exercise 1.11

Remembering a Memorable Live Theater Experience

Directions: Think about the most enjoyable time you have spent attending a *live* theater performance. Your example could be a children's theater production, a school or community theater performance, or professional drama that you have seen.

Tell about the aspects of the experience you remember most. What do you think made these elements so memorable? How did the fact that the performance was "live" contribute to your experience of it?

_____

_____

_____

_____

_____

_____

_____

_____

_____

_____

_____

_____

_____

_____

_____

_____

_____

Name _____   Date _____

Film and Television Drama

Experiencing a performance on film or television does not include the  direct performer-to-audience feedback of live theater. Yet the medium of film and the medium of television each have their own special techniques to communicate powerful drama.

The Medium of Film

First, let's consider the medium of **film**. What are some capabilities of drama that film does best?

For one thing, film can offer a realism that exceeds any that can be achieved on stage. A stage play can only pretend to take audiences to a specific place; film can actually take you there.

Film crews can film on location almost anywhere: the Grand Canyon, the streets of San Francisco, etc. Films such as *Gandhi* or *The English Patient* benefit greatly from being filmed at real-life sites. Film can even create realistic locations to resemble the real thing.

Example	For a Civil War scene in the movie *Gone With the Wind,* the filmmakers created a replica of the city of Atlanta—in order to burn it!

A second advantage has to do with the fact that film is a medium that is edited. A director can work with actors in a scene and have them act the scene over and over until it is just right. The scene is not printed until it is perfect. On the live stage, an actor can have an off day. In film, bad performances can be literally thrown away.

Think about your favorite film performances. They are now captured forever because the film director was able to work to get the "best" from the actors. We are lucky, too, that the medium of film allows us a permanent record of those performances. In contrast, a brilliant stage performance can only last in the memories of those who saw it.

A third quality of the film medium is also involved with editing. The final version of a film that you see on the screen is actually comprised of a number of shots. These are combined to tell the film's story. The next time you watch a film, keep track of how often the camera's point of view shifts. Sometimes the camera is very close to the actor's face (called a "close-up"). Sometimes the camera photographs the scene from far away, even from a helicopter or plane.

After all the scenes of a film have been shot, it becomes the editor's job to piece selected shots together to tell the story in the very best way. Although the viewer is usually not aware of the editor's choices, the overall effect has a powerful impact on our experience of the film. Every year, when an Academy Award is given out for Best Editor, examples of the editor's art are shown. One obvious way in which the editor's contribution is shown is the way action and chase scenes are assembled.

Example	In the movie *The Fugitive,* the action scenes are edited to create the greatest possible suspense.

(continued)

Drama: A Comprehensive Guide to Dramatic Elements and Style

Name _____ Date _____

Film and Television Drama *(continued)*

Finally, consider the role that sound effects and music play in a film. Vivid sounds such as car tires squealing, glass breaking, and explosions add realism to the experience of any film. Film music also has an important effect on the mood. It subtly manipulates your feelings toward characters and plot developments.

Example	In the *Star Wars* movies, a distinctive crashing noise is heard each time the light sabers clash.

The Medium of Television

The dramatic medium of **television** shares many of the same technical qualities of film. In fact, most of the drama programs shown on television—both weekly series and made-for-TV movies—are filmed in exactly the same way as feature films shown in a movie theater. Does the television medium offer any special qualities of its own?

One possible difference is the fact that some TV programs (soap operas, for instance) are photographed on video tape, not film. Such programs are taped in advance and electronically edited. However, the overall effect is that the action on the screen is happening live. Could this illusion of being "realer" than filmed drama contribute to the popularity of such long-running soap operas as *Days of Our Lives* or *General Hospital*?

Another characteristic that is special in television is the "laff track" that is sometimes added to situation comedies. Sometimes the laughter is real, since the show has been recorded in front of a live audience. Sometimes the laughter is artificial, having been electronically added as a laff track. This is designed to encourage viewers at home to laugh at comic moments in the dialogue and action. Some television critics argue that television comedy should stand by itself. The home viewer should be the one to decide what's funny. How do you react when you hear laughter accompanying a sitcom? Can you recognize the difference between real and canned laughter?

If you were writing a script for television, you'd have to write your script to include interruptions for commercials. Have you ever noticed how your favorite programs are written to a formula? The commercial breaks occur in the program at the same intervals each week.

Writing a one hour police drama, for instance, is somewhat like writing a four-act play. Each quarter takes the plot a bit further while ending on a dramatic note. This is designed to make the viewer want to stay tuned after the commercial. With the competition of programs on other channels, the television writer has to work hard to keep the viewer interested. It's so easy—and tempting—just to change the channel!

Drama: A Comprehensive Guide
to Dramatic Elements and Style

Name _____   Date _____

 *Exercise 1.12*

Film and TV Study

When you watch film or TV drama, you often get so caught up in the story that you lose awareness of aspects of the medium through which the story is being presented. These experiments will help you become more aware of the special qualities of film and television.

Directions

1. To become more aware of the *editing* of film and TV drama, study a small portion of a film (as recorded on video) and/or TV program. Turn off the sound, so that you can concentrate fully on the visuals.

   Then count the "cuts" (changes in camera angle) that occur within an interval of two minutes. Try studying a sample from another drama. Is the number of cuts the same? If not, can you explain why not?

   _____

   _____

   _____

2. Continue watching—with the sound off—for another two minutes. This time, focus on how the restrictiveness of the camera eye dictates what you can, and cannot, see from moment to moment.

   Ask yourself as you watch, why do you think the editor chose this particular combination of shots with which to present the drama?

   _____

   _____

   _____

3. Now, turn on the sound again. Study a scene from a film in which music and/or sound effects play an important role. How is sound used to manipulate the feelings or thoughts of the viewer?

   _____

   _____

   _____

Drama: A Comprehensive Guide
to Dramatic Elements and Style

Name _____   Date _____

 Exercise 1.13

Converting Fiction to Drama in Different Media

Directions: Work in pairs on the same creative "think tank" assignment: "If you were to produce the well-known fairy tale *Little Red Riding Hood* for live theater, film, and TV, how might your choices *differ* for each medium?"

What approaches would you emphasize in each medium to make the most of that medium? Compare your team's ideas with those of other teams.

Live Theater _____

_____

_____

_____

_____

Film _____

_____

_____

_____

_____

Television _____

_____

_____

_____

_____

Part 2: Basic Tools—
Elements of Drama

Objectives

1. To introduce students to essential concepts in the critical vocabulary of drama;

2. To provide students with opportunities to apply these concepts critically in the analysis of contemporary drama;

3. To offer students opportunities to explore these concepts creatively.

Teaching Tips

Although reading examples for the concepts introduced in this unit are most often drawn from stage drama, the teacher is encouraged to interpret the notion of "drama" to include film and television drama. Continue to help students to make connections between these formal concepts and their current popular personal viewing.

Appendix A offers a reproducible definition list of all drama vocabulary included throughout this text. Appendices C and D provide students interested in scriptwriting with generic "format" pages for writing playscripts and screenplays. Sample pages are included to show students how a specific script might look using the conventions introduced on the format pages.

At any point, student actors might be encouraged to perform original script materials written by themselves or other dramatists in the class.

For artistically oriented students, the section on Setting offers opportunities for nonverbal follow-up activities, such as drawing or constructing models for original stage settings.

Warm-up Activity

Use Trash Theater to introduce your students to the elements of drama discussed in this unit: *conflict, character, dialogue, setting, plot,* and *dramatic structure.* Trash Theater also introduces student actors to the notion of *improvisation*—the ability to make up a play on the spot.

To prepare, ask each student to bring from home two ordinary items—a pocket comb, a left boot, an old book, a toilet plunger, etc. Before performance day, randomly separate the collected objects into separate "prop" bags, each containing five or six items.

Divide the class into teams of four students each and give each team a prop bag. Each team now has 15 minutes to plan—and to practice (briefly)—an instant play to perform for the rest of the class.

There are two main rules. Each play *must* include *all* the props that the group has been given—though props may be used in nontraditional ways. Also, *each* team member must have a part in the skit.

When all teams have performed, ask the class to discuss which of the skits were funniest, most convincing, etc. What do the results of this exercise suggest about what makes effective drama?

(continued)

Part 2: Basic Tools—
Elements of Drama *(continued)*

Extension Activities

- <u>Studying Conflict in Real Life:</u> Extend your students' study of conflict in drama by asking them to look for conflict in their own lives. How would a dramatist turn the raw material of their own personal conflicts—with friends, siblings, parents, etc.—into effective drama? Students may attempt to turn such material from their own lives into actual scripted scenes.

- <u>Real Life Speech vs. Dramatic Dialogue:</u> Although dramatic dialogue *seems* very realistic, it is actually quite unlike the way we *really* talk. A vivid demonstration of this can be realized by having students tape record—and then transcribe—an actual conversation between friends. Make sure students ask permission before recording. Once the transcript is finished, ask students to turn the dialogue into dramatic dialogue. Have them note what editing processes are required to make the transformation.

- <u>Radio Drama:</u> Students can learn a great deal about the elements of drama by listening to recordings of famous radio dramas. Without the visual element, they can focus specifically on vocal characterizations, the role of sound effects and music, etc. Students may even choose to create their own radio dramas to perform live or record.

Name _____   Date _____

Conflict

At the center of all drama—tragedy or comedy—is **conflict**. Conflict is the "skeleton" on which any drama is built. Without conflict there is no central action to hold the interest of the audience.

Different types of conflict can be dramatized. Most often, there is conflict *between characters,* or *between groups of characters.*

Example	In Shakespeare's *Romeo and Juliet,* the love between Romeo and Juliet is threatened, and finally destroyed, by the conflict between their families.

Conflict Between Characters

If the central conflict between characters involves characters who are not evenly matched, audiences tend to side with the underdog. In this way, the playwright draws the audience into caring about the outcome.

Example	In Tennessee Williams's *The Glass Menagerie,* the audience sympathizes with shy, crippled Laura.

Some dramas clearly involve a conflict between a "good" hero we identify with and a "bad" villain we dislike. The main character in such a drama is called the **protagonist**. The character who opposes the main character is called the **antagonist**.

Conflict Between a Character and Outside Forces

Second, conflict can also occur between one character and outside forces such as fate or destiny, society, or the supernatural.

Example	In Sophocles's *Oedipus the King,* Oedipus, without knowing who they are, kills his father and marries his mother. He is trapped by a fate he cannot control.

Conflict Within a Character

Third, there can be conflict within a character. This involves a struggle between a character and himself, such as a conflict of desires, values, or motives.

Example	In Shakespeare's *Hamlet,* Hamlet learns that his father was killed by his own brother. His inner conflicts keep him from taking revenge during the whole course of the play.

Mixed Conflict

Of course, many dramas include more than one type of conflict. For example, a character could hate another character (conflict between characters) and also hate herself for how she feels (conflict within a character).

Consider the mixture of conflicts in Arthur Miller's drama, *Death of a Salesman.* The main character, salesman Willy Loman, faces the outer conflict of rejection by former business contacts. He also faces the inner realization of the decay of his life dreams. In addition, his sons Happy and Biff must grapple with their own conflicts about accepting—and forgiving—the weaknesses of their father.

Name _____   Date _____

 Exercise 2.1

Conflict in Television Scripts

Directions: Think about episodes of three different TV shows (drama or comedy) that you have watched recently. Name the program and briefly describe the central **conflict** in the episode you have chosen.

Then list the category that each central conflict best fits into:

> 1. Conflict between characters
> 2. Conflict between one character and outside forces
> 3. Conflict within a character
> 4. Mixed conflict

Program 1

Title: _____

Description of Central Conflict: _____

_____

_____

Conflict Category: _____

Program 2

Title: _____

Description of Central Conflict: _____

_____

_____

Conflict Category: _____

Program 3

Title: _____

Description of Central Conflict: _____

_____

_____

Conflict Category: _____

*Drama: A Comprehensive Guide
to Dramatic Elements and Style*

Name _____   Date _____

 *Exercise 2.2*

Plot Your Own Conflicts

Directions: Make up *two* examples of each of the four types of conflict described in the reading as they might be dramatized in your own original play, film, or TV script.

Conflict 1: Between characters

Example 1: _____

_____

Example 2: _____

_____

Conflict 2: Between one character and outside forces

Example 1: _____

_____

Example 2: _____

_____

Conflict 3: Within a character

Example 1: _____

_____

Example 2: _____

_____

Conflict 4: Mixed conflict

Example 1: _____

_____

Example 2: _____

_____

> **Discussion Question:** Which category of conflict do you think makes the most interesting drama? Explain your answer to the class.

*Drama: A Comprehensive Guide
to Dramatic Elements and Style*

Name _____   Date _____

Character

Interesting characters are essential ingredients in a satisfying drama. One good definition of drama is "character in action," because the unfolding action of the plot is affected so much by the specific characters involved.

Unlike a character in a novel, a character in a dramatic script is revealed through just a limited number of scenes. The dramatist communicates a character's identity with a minimum of dialogue, gestures, and actions.

The Character's Appearance

 The dramatist communicates the nature of a character to the audience in many ways. One method is through the character's appearance—how a character looks and moves on stage.

Example	In Shakespeare's *Richard III*, the title character is a villain. His physical deformity—a hunchback—reflects his deformed mind. The actor must choose how to show the handicap in the character's gestures and movements.

The Character's Speech

A second method of creating character is through the way a character talks. The language that characters use to communicate their thoughts and feelings tells the audience a great deal about who they are.

Example	In Edmond Rostand's play *Cyrano de Bergerac*, the title character is distinguished not only by his huge nose but also by his great flair for words.

The Character's Behavior

A third method of creating character is through the way a character behaves. Audiences study the choices a character makes in relating to others.

Example	In the musical play *Don Quixote*, the title character misinterprets events, but his courage gives courage to others.

A well-drawn character has a background of feelings, beliefs, needs, hurts, and unsatisfied desires. These are often hidden from the audience, from other characters, and sometimes from the character himself or herself at the start of the drama.

Part of the excitement of much drama is the slow process by which the audience begins to see deeper and deeper into a character. Bit by bit, we come to understand the secret needs that motivate the character's actions as the drama unfolds. One example is the classic film *Citizen Kane*.

Example	Orson Welles's movie *Citizen Kane* opens with the death of the main character, newspaperman Charles Foster Kane. The film then tells Kane's story in a series of flashbacks. It isn't until the very end that the last piece of the puzzle explains the inner life of Kane's complex character.

The most interesting characters are often people of contradictions. Just like people in real life, realistic characters have conflicting feelings about choices. Often, like us, they desire conflicting things at the same time.

Name _____   Date _____

 Exercise 2.3

Complete a Character Profile

Directions: Choose a character from stage, screen, or TV whom you find interesting. Write a Character Profile by answering the questions below.

Character's Name: _____

From which play, film, or TV program: _____

Describe how your character looks (physical characteristics, style of dress, etc.): _____

_____

_____

_____

Describe how your character moves (the way he/she walks, characteristic gestures, etc.):

_____

_____

_____

_____

Describe how your character talks (voice characteristics, style of language, etc.): _____

_____

_____

Describe how your character behaves (choices he/she makes, what other characters say about

him/her, etc.): _____

_____

_____

Tell about any interesting contradictions or hidden needs that motivate his or her behavior:

_____

_____

_____

Name _____ Date _____

Exercise 2.4

Portray Someone You Know As a Character in a Drama

If you were a dramatist, how would you portray **yourself**, a **friend**, or a **family member** as a character in a stage, film, or television drama?

Think about what important characteristics you would include. How would you communicate them to an audience?

Directions: Describe how the person you have chosen would look, move, talk, and behave on stage. What interesting contradictions or hidden needs might you include in your character sketch?

_____

_____

_____

_____

_____

_____

_____

_____

_____

_____

_____

_____

_____

_____

_____

_____

_____

Name _____ Date _____

Dialogue

In most dramas, dialogue is an important element. It is used by dramatists to portray character and to dramatize conflict.

To Show Background

One important function of dialogue is to allow playwrights to show the characters' backgrounds to the audience. Characters communicate a great deal about themselves by both how they speak and what they say. A character's manner of speaking—accent, rhythm, tone, choice of words—gives important clues about his or her background. By listening carefully, the audience can learn a great deal about a character's identity.

A master of using dialogue for this purpose is the American playwright Tennessee Williams.

Example	In *A Streetcar Named Desire,* Williams uses dialogue to arouse both love and pity for Blanche Dubois, the troubled sister.

To Show Inner Thoughts

Second, dialogue can be used to reveal a character's inner thoughts and feelings. The volume and rhythm of a character's speech often reveal a great deal about how he or she is thinking or feeling. Nonverbal clues—such as facial expressions, postures, and gestures—can also communicate a character's true thoughts and feelings.

To Communicate

A third important function of dialogue is to allow characters to communicate with each other. One definition of dialogue is "personality in action." Dialogue is the medium by which characters relate—or do not relate—to each other. Dialogue is an important way that dramatists can dramatize conflict between characters. In well-written dialogue, words have force. Characters use words to persuade, convince, and assert their power over each other.

Example	In Edward Albee's *Who's Afraid of Virginia Woolf,* characters use words to intimidate, infuriate, and overpower each other.

Text and Subtext

In many scenes, the "true" dialogue goes on *below* the spoken words. For instance, characters who seem to be talking politely about the weather may actually be engaging in a furious argument. When a character says one thing but is really thinking or feeling something else, actors call the character's "real" message the **subtext**.

The Power of Silence

Conflict in dialogue doesn't always rely on words. Silence can communicate powerfully, too. The contemporary British playwright Harold Pinter, for example, has developed a style of dialogue that uses pauses between spoken lines. His plays dramatize the power struggles that show audiences how many sub-messages lie under the most innocent exchanges between characters.

Drama: A Comprehensive Guide to Dramatic Elements and Style

Name _____   Date _____

 Exercise 2.5

Fun with Subtext

Directions: Think about an everyday situation in which characters might speak to each other in one way while really thinking quite different thoughts.

First, write a short dialogue that contains the words that the characters actually say to each other. On your paper, leave a blank line under each line of dialogue. (Follow the format suggested below.)

Now, beneath each line of dialogue that you have written, write the "subtext" dialogue which contains the thoughts and feelings that each character does *not* express—but is actually thinking or feeling—in the situation.

	Sample Subtext Dialogue
Jack: [Subtext:]	(Cautiously) Hello, Jill. It's been a long time. *After all this time, she still looks beautiful.*
Jill: [Subtext:]	(Truly surprised) Hi Jack . . . *I can't believe my heart is racing. I'm still not over him!*
Jack: [Subtext:]	(Flippantly) Well, how long has it been? *Who are you kidding, Jack? You know <u>exactly</u>—3 years, 3 months, and 2 days . . .*
Jill: [Subtext:]	(Also lightly) It's been a while. *I've missed him so much. Why did we let that fight end it all?*
Jack: [Subtext:]	(A bit nervously) So, what are you up to now, Jill? *Please, please don't say that you're married.*
Jill: [Subtext:]	My job takes me all over the world. How about you? *Could it be true? Does he still care about <u>us</u>?*
Jack: [Subtext:]	(Laughs falsely) I still work here in town. *Is there still a chance we might make it after all?*
Jill: [Subtext:] [etc.]	(Tentatively) What a coincidence we met today . . . *Do I dare to suggest we go out for coffee?*

Drama: A Comprehensive Guide
to Dramatic Elements and Style

Name _____   Date _____

Exercise 2.6

How We Communicate with Body Language

Are you aware that characters in drama—and people in real life—speak continuously, even when they are silent? Our body language often reveals to others what we are really thinking and feeling, even when we are unaware of those thoughts and feelings ourselves.

Directions: Spend a day observing people—friends, family members, and strangers. Look at facial expressions, the way people stand, the way they use their hands, etc. Carry a small notebook and record the different ways in which you see people communicating with their bodies, either when they are with others or when they are alone.

In the space below, note five of the behaviors you have seen and what you believe they express about how the person was feeling or thinking. Compare your list with the lists of other students in your class.

Behavior	Interpretation
Example: man in doctor's office crosses and uncrosses legs	nervous about his appointment
1.	
2.	
3.	
4.	
5.	

Drama: A Comprehensive Guide
to Dramatic Elements and Style

Name _____   Date _____

Setting

Just as in a short story or novel, the **setting** of a drama can play an important role in shaping the action of the play and how the audience responds to it.

Establish Place and Time

One obvious but very important function of setting is that it places the drama in a specific place and time. Every plot is affected in major and minor ways by the place and time in which it takes place.

Example	Shakespeare's *Julius Caesar,* set in ancient Rome, tells of the murder of a powerful politician. Think how the story would change if it were set in Washington, D.C.

Backdrops, costumes, and props would be different. And the essentials of character and situation would be significantly affected by taking place in modern America, not ancient Rome.

Establish Mood

Second, the setting of a drama also contributes to the mood of the play. Qualities of light, sound, and color have an effect on characters within the drama. They also affect the audience watching it. Think about how different a plot about passengers stranded after a plane crash would "feel" depending on whether it was set in an Arctic blizzard or in a sun-scorched desert. How

would each atmosphere affect the interaction of the characters, as well as the experience of the viewers?

Place Drama Within a Culture

Third, the specific culture of a drama's setting directly affects the attitudes and behavior of characters. Often, the culture associated with a setting contains its own set of values, traditions, and expectations of behavior. Specific characters in the drama may or may not feel comfortable with these.

Example	In the movie *The Gods Must Be Crazy,* a Kalahari bushman leaves the desert on a mission. The contrast between the Kalahari and the world outside contributes to the plot development.

Reflect Characters' Feelings

Finally, in some plays, dramatists place characters in settings specifically designed to reflect their innermost thoughts and feelings. Nonrealistic, surrealistic (dreamlike) scenery—such as geometric shapes or melting buildings—may be used. Such a setting suggests complicated feelings, dreams, or even madness inside the characters' minds.

One playwright known for using such settings is Samuel Beckett.

Example	His play *Happy Days* opens with a woman talking happily while buried in earth up to her waist. This setting symbolizes the possibilities of true communication between people.

Name _____ Date _____

Exercise 2.7

The Uses of Setting in Horror Films

Setting often plays a key role in the genre of horror films.

Directions: Think about a horror film in which the element of setting was important. Answer the questions below to help you understand the functions that setting plays in the film.

Name of film: _____

How was setting used to establish the specific time and place of the story?

_____

_____

_____

How was setting used to create mood? How did this mood affect the characters in the drama? What effect did the mood have on you and other viewers?

_____

_____

_____

Did the setting take place in a specific culture with values, traditions, or expectations that affected the characters? Explain.

_____

_____

_____

Did the setting in any way seem to reflect the innermost thoughts and feelings of characters in the film? Explain.

_____

_____

_____

Name _____   Date _____

Exercise 2.8

Invent Your Own Play Setting

Without actually writing a play, imagine your own stage drama in which the setting would play a major role in the characters'—and audience's—experience of the drama.

Directions: First, briefly describe your play's plot. Then, describe the setting as you imagine it to appear on stage. Finally, describe in what ways *your* setting functions in ways similar to the four functions described in the reading:

1. establishing time and place;
2. establishing mood;
3. placing the drama within a specific culture; and
4. reflecting the innermost thoughts and feelings of characters.

_____

_____

_____

_____

_____

_____

_____

_____

_____

_____

_____

_____

_____

_____

_____

Name _____   Date _____

Plot

The **plot** of a drama is its "story." Plot consists of the important events that occur during the course of the play. Plot also includes background events that have led up to the present action.

Dramatic Unity

A good plot must have **dramatic unity**. All the actions must relate to the central conflict(s). A satisfying plot introduces a core problem, complicates that problem, and then resolves it—though not always happily.

Example	The movie *Tootsie*. An actor can't find work. (core problem) He dresses up as a woman and gets a part, then falls in love with another woman on the show. (complication) Other men are drawn to the "actress" he plays. (more complication) The truth is revealed and he and his love are united. (resolution)

Dramatic Change

Plot almost always involves change. If a play begins on a quiet note, for instance, something happens very soon to set the plot in motion. Whatever change occurs, circumstances are rarely the same at the end of the drama as they were at the beginning.

There are many kinds of dramatic change. One cause of change is external

circumstances. A hurricane hits. An illness strikes. An accident happens. These are all events that are outside the characters' direct control.

Example	In the film *The Wizard of Oz*, a tornado takes Dorothy from Kansas to Oz.

Another cause of change is the consequence of a character's action. A character's decision—or indecision—can set in motion a chain of events in the plot.

Example	In Shakespeare's *Macbeth*, events are set in motion when Macbeth decides to kill the king, and acts on his decision.

(continued)

*Drama: A Comprehensive Guide
to Dramatic Elements and Style*

Name _____   Date _____

Plot *(continued)*

Changes in relationships also drive plots. Think of all the plots that involve characters who fall in—or out of—love. Love is a powerful force in drama. Characters in love may commit selfless acts they would never have risked before. Love can also bring out the darker side of characters. Many plots revolve around feelings such as jealousy, envy, and even revenge.

Take a look at film plots you know that involve strong feelings in relationships.

Example	In the movie *Kramer vs. Kramer,* two estranged parents fight bitterly over custody of their son.

Perhaps the most satisfying kind of plot is one that leads to a positive change in attitude of an important character. Many plots focus on a character who makes a change for the better as a result of learning important life lessons.

Example	In *A Christmas Carol,* Ebenezer Scrooge changes from a cold miser to a warm and giving man.

Whatever the nature of change that it contains, any successful plot must hold the audience's interest. We must have good reason to care about the story's characters. We must also find the events in the plot believable.

Name _____ Date _____

 *Exercise 2.9*

Studying Television Plots

Most dramatic plots involve change. The situation at the end of the drama is different from the situation at the beginning.

Directions: Think about episodes of three different TV shows (drama or comedy) that you have watched recently. For each, tell the name of the program. Next, describe how the situation of the plot is different at the end from beginning. Then, explain the key factor(s) in the plot which led to that change.

Title of Program #1: _____

Change in plot situation: _____

_____

_____

Cause(s) of change: _____

_____

_____

Title of Program #2: _____

Change in plot situation: _____

_____

_____

Cause(s) of change: _____

_____

_____

Title of Program #3: _____

Change in plot situation: _____

_____

_____

Cause(s) of change: _____

_____

_____

Drama: A Comprehensive Guide
to Dramatic Elements and Style

Name _____   Date _____

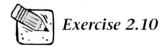 *Exercise 2.10*

What Makes a Good Plot?

Directions: List four plays, films, or TV programs that you consider to have particularly satisfying plots. Explain what you think makes each of these plots effective.

Plot #1: _____

_____

_____

_____

Plot #2: _____

_____

_____

_____

Plot #3: _____

_____

_____

_____

Plot #4: _____

_____

_____

_____

Now, review your answers. What elements do your favorite plots have in common?

_____

_____

_____

Drama: A Comprehensive Guide
to Dramatic Elements and Style

Name _____   Date _____

Dramatic Structure

Have you ever heard someone spoil a great joke by telling it in the wrong order? The same is true for a great plot. The order in which the parts of a plot are presented is as important as the story itself.

A major element of dramatic structure is how the playwright introduces, complicates, and resolves the major conflict(s) of the plot over the length of the play. The following five terms are often used to describe the key parts of a drama's structure.

Exposition

Exposition is the way the playwright communicates information about the background of the characters. This can include events that took place before the start of the play. It can also contain information about the characters' relationships with each other. A skilled playwright knows how to work in background information without making it seem obvious. The audience is allowed to learn facts that they need at the same time that the present action is advancing.

Point of Attack

The **point of attack** is the moment in the plot when an important chain of events is set in motion. This leads to the core conflict(s) in the plot. This may be a moment in which a character makes a momentous decision that allows for no going back.

Example	In the movie *Rain Man,* the adventure begins when the younger brother kidnaps his older brother from the institution.

Complication

The **complication** introduces new plot elements that affect the course of action of the play.

Example	A new character may be introduced, or a secret may be revealed.

These elements increase the dramatic tension of the building conflict(s).

Example	In Arthur Miller's *Death of a Salesman,* a flashback shows Biff learning that his father has been unfaithful to his mother.

Climax

The **climax** is that dramatic moment (or series of moments) when the conflict(s) come to a head. This is an exciting time in any plot and usually has been prepared for by much rising dramatic tension.

Example	In Lawrence and Lee's *Inherit the Wind,* the climax comes when defense lawyer Drummond puts evangelist Matthew Brady on the witness stand.

(continued)

Drama: A Comprehensive Guide to Dramatic Elements and Style

Name _____   Date _____

Dramatic Structure *(continued)*

Resolution

Finally, the **resolution** is the conclusion of the plot. It contains the final solution of the play's central conflict(s). It is usually much quieter than the climax.

Example	In *Inherit the Wind,* the resolution comes as Drummond, leaving the empty courtroom, picks up both the Bible and Darwin's *The Origin of Species* and places them together in his briefcase.

In the best-structured dramas, the exposition leads logically all the way to the resolution. Skillful playwrights create continued suspense by keeping the audience guessing about what will happen next and how things will turn out at the end.

Name _____ Date _____

 Exercise 2.11

Diagramming a Plot

The plots of stage, film, and television dramas do not always fit perfectly neatly into the pattern of **exposition**, **point of attack**, **complication**, **climax**, and **resolution** presented in the reading. However, by looking for these key elements, you can begin to recognize the dramatic structure that supports every effective plot.

Directions: Choose a stage, film, or television drama that you believe to have a particularly effective plot. (Preferably choose a drama that you own in script or videotape form so that you can study it closely.) In the spaces below, describe where parts of the drama you have chosen fit into the five elements of dramatic structure that you have studied.

Drama Title: _____

1. **Exposition:** _____

_____

_____

2. **Point of attack:** _____

_____

_____

3. **Complication:** _____

_____

_____

4. **Climax:** _____

_____

_____

5. **Resolution:** _____

_____

_____

Drama: A Comprehensive Guide
to Dramatic Elements and Style

Name _____   Date _____

 Exercise 2.12

Turn a Newspaper Story into a Dramatic Plot Structure

Some of today's most compelling dramas are drawn from real-life events. Try your own hand at turning fact into fiction—and learning more about dramatic structure at the same time.

Directions: First, find a newspaper story about an actual person or situation that interests you. Imagine that you are going to turn this real story into a drama for stage, screen, or TV.

Think about how you would "borrow" elements of the actual newspaper account to make good drama. Tell what elements you would include in each of the five plot structure categories below. How will the medium you choose (stage, screen, or TV) affect the choices you make?

1. **Exposition:** _____

   _____

   _____

2. **Point of attack:** _____

   _____

   _____

3. **Complication:** _____

   _____

   _____

4. **Climax:** _____

   _____

   _____

5. **Resolution:** _____

   _____

   _____

*Drama: A Comprehensive Guide
to Dramatic Elements and Style*

Part 3:
Other Dramatic Tools—
Appreciating Plays as Literature

Objectives

1. To help students develop the skills necessary to enjoy reading playscripts;

2. To expose students to additional critical concepts particularly involved with appreciating drama as literature;

3. To introduce students to the conventions and traditions associated with five different genres of drama: tragedy, melodrama, comedy, satire, and farce.

Teaching Tips

Learning to read drama can be very difficult, especially for students who are not skilled readers or who do not have experience attending live theater performances. It's important for teachers to sympathize with those difficulties.

Be careful about reading plays aloud in class. Don't fall into the rut of having students take turns reading the text, line by line, day after day. Focus on a few key dramatic scenes, rather than on a complete in-class reading of the entire play. (Also, if you tend to be a bit of a "ham," be careful not to read too much of the play aloud yourself.)

Students of all learning styles are generally quite interested in comedy genres. Encourage the use of comic dramatic skills in your class. Perhaps one or more of your nonacademic students will turn "class clown" tendencies into comic acting or writing talents.

Warm-up Activity

Initiate an honest class discussion about the difficulties that your students have encountered previously in reading drama in script form.

What plays have they already read? Which plays were hardest to read? Which were easiest? Why?

What strategies have students discovered to help them to enjoy the process of reading plays more? What can you share about your own play reading experiences?

Extension Activities

• Propaganda on Stage: Divide the class into groups of three or four. Each group is to write, practice, and perform a short skit designed to affect the audience's thinking about a specific current issue. (Groups can choose their own issues to dramatize or dramatize ideas found in newspaper articles or editorials of special interest.) Each presentation should make use of propaganda tactics designed to influence the audience to favor one side of the issue—even if obvious balanced arguments could be made for both sides.

(continued)

Part 3: Other Dramatic Tools— Appreciating Plays as Literature *(continued)*

- Plan Your Own Tragic Drama Plot: For centuries, playwrights have been writing tragic dramas that explore deep questions about the nature of fate, justice, and suffering. Ask students, working alone or in pairs, to compose a "modern" tragic drama plot. What themes do they think would be most relevant for contemporary audiences? What kind of character today might qualify as a tragic hero in such a plot? Ask students to write out a plot description for their tragedies and then compare results with the rest of the class.

- Parody in Drama: The films of Mel Brooks offer hilarious examples of dramatic parodies of well-known cowboy, monster, space, and suspense genres, among others. Break up your class into small groups, and invite each group to compose a short comic skit that parodies a familiar plot or genre. (Some might even tackle a parody of a "serious" play that the class has been reading.) After each parody is performed for the rest of the class, invite students to talk about what elements from the original plot have been retained and what elements have been distorted for comic effect.

- Stage a Debate: Help students organize a debate focussing on the merits of the genre of formal tragedy versus the genre of popular melodrama. Have opposing teams debate a resolution that compares a well-known melodrama (play, film, or TV drama) with a famous tragic drama (e.g. "RESOLVED: *The Godfather* is better entertainment than *Macbeth*"). Help them build arguments for each side involving concepts introduced in the reading.

Name _____ Date _____

Learning to Read Drama

Many dramas are published in text form so that they can be enjoyed on the page as well as on stage. Like fiction and poetry, most of the plays that you read in school are studied in the category of "literature." Learning to make a dramatic script come to life in your imagination as you read it takes some practice.

Reading a dramatic script is different from reading a short story or a novel. Novelists and short story writers can communicate with readers in ways that dramatists cannot. For example, fiction writers can include description to help establish characters or settings in the reader's mind. Playwrights tell their stories primarily in the dialogue and stage action.

A second difference is that the novelists and short story writers can quickly and easily switch from scene to scene. Sometimes fiction jumps from scene to scene in just a page or two. The stage dramatist is confined by stage space as well as by the time involved to change scenes. A playwright must develop the story in fewer scenes.

A third difference is that the fiction writer can use specific points of view. The use of a narrator or omniscient point of view allows the reader to get inside the thoughts of characters. Some stage dramas make use of a narrator. For the most part, however, the stage dramatist must rely on characters to speak for themselves. The audience is left to interpret the inner life of characters from what they say and do.

For these reasons and more, reading a dramatic script requires special skills. With little description and only the playwright's stage directions as clues, it's up to the reader to imagine the setting, the main characters, and the action.

Visualize the Script

Here's one technique you might find helpful in bringing a script alive in your mind. Visualize, as clearly as possible, what you would be seeing on stage if you were attending an actual performance. When you come to beginnings of acts or scene changes, don't skip over the author's description of the stage setting. Read the instructions carefully. Try to picture how a set designer might translate the author's wishes into reality. Also, pay careful attention to the clues the playwright provides to describe the characters. Make a mental image of their physical appearance, how they are dressed, the props they may be carrying, etc. Try to create a detailed picture of each character in your mind as you read the dialogue.

(continued)

Drama: A Comprehensive Guide to Dramatic Elements and Style

Name _____   Date _____

Learning to Read Drama *(continued)*

Stage Directions

Pay attention, too, to the playwright's notes about stage action. Try to keep track of where characters are on stage. Then move them in your mind according to the play-wright's stage directions.

The term "downstage" means toward the audience (see diagram below). "Upstage" means away from the audience. (This is because early stages were slanted so that characters in back of other characters—upstage—could still be seen by the audience.) The terms "stage right" and "stage left" are written from the point of view of the actor on stage, facing the audience. When an actor moves stage right, from the audience's point of view, the character moves to the left.

Finally, since a play consists mostly of dialogue, you—the reader—must also provide the voices yourself. As you read, try to hear in your mind how each character sounds. Playwrights often provide script directions for how a certain line should be read by the actor.

Stage scripts, as well as scripts for film and television, are written with certain conventions. Eventually, reading scripts will be as comfortable and enjoyable as reading your favorite short stories or novels.

Rear of stage

stage right

downstage

upstage

stage left

Audience

Drama: A Comprehensive Guide
to Dramatic Elements and Style

Name _____   Date _____

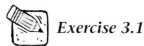 *Exercise 3.1*

Bringing a Script to Life in Your Imagination

Your imagination—your ability to visualize pictures in your mind and your ability to hear sounds—is a great tool for helping you to enjoy reading plays. Like all skills, reading drama scripts with your imagination takes practice.

Directions: Choose a play script that you have never seen in performance—or read—before. Open to the first page of the first scene of the play and slowly work through the questions below.

1. **Setting**

   * If the dramatist tells the **time** and **place** of the opening scene, note them here:

   _____

   _____

   * Draw a rough sketch—from the audience's point of view—of how the stage setting is described. (Remember that directions such as "stage left" are written from the actor's perspective and need to be reversed for the audience.) Be sure to include all items described, including furniture, props, etc.

2. **Characters**

   * Make a quick sketch of each of the characters described at the opening of the scene. (Add other sketches for characters who enter later in the scene.) What does the dramatist tell about their physical characteristics? how they are dressed?

   * Beneath each character sketch, write the character's name and any other descriptive material that has been provided.

(continued)

Drama: A Comprehensive Guide to Dramatic Elements and Style

Name _____ Date _____

Bringing a Script to Life in Your Imagination *(continued)*

3. Opening Stage Picture

* Imagine sitting in the audience when the play begins; sketch what the opening "stage picture" would look like. Which characters are on stage? Where are they placed? What are they doing?

* If there are music or sound effects, note them here: _____

_____

_____

4. Dialogue

* When each character speaks, take time to imagine what his or her voice would sound like. Describe your impression of each character's voice qualities here:

_____

_____

_____

_____

_____

_____

* What clues does the playwright give about how specific lines of dialogue are to be spoken? When an instruction is given, take time to "hear" the character actually speaking the line in this way. List a few of such instructions here:

_____

_____

_____

_____

_____

5. Stage Action

* What does the playwright tell about the actions and movements of the characters? When the script indicates that a character changes position on the stage, actually visualize the move taking place in your imagination.

Drama: A Comprehensive Guide
to Dramatic Elements and Style

Name _____ Date _____

Imagery and Symbolism

In many ways, a dramatic script shares similarities with a poem. Like poetry, drama presents a concentrated version of reality. Drama focuses on the most essential parts to present its story.

Imagery

Like poets, dramatists sometimes use imagery to communicate complex feelings and ideas. **Imagery** can be defined as descriptive language that makes use of similes or metaphors.

One way that dramatists use imagery is to portray elements of the setting. Dramatists can use poetic language to expand the scope of the actual stage settings.

For example, the theater of Shakespeare's day had little scenery or special effects. Shakespeare used the power of word images to help his audience picture an imagined backdrop.

 Exercise 3.2

Imagery

One challenge for the dramatist who wants to use imagery in a play is that it needs to be given in dialogue. A novelist can describe a beautiful scene using picturesque language. A playwright has to use words that a character can say and still sound believable.

Directions: These two descriptions are written the way they might appear in a novel. Rewrite them so that they could be spoken in a play or movie.

Example	The setting sun stained the water blood-red and cast lurid shadows around Jem and Anya. The argument continued.
	In dialogue:
	Anya: Jem, let's go in. I don't want to sit here any more.
	Jem: I'm not going in till I get an answer.
	Anya: It's creepy out here at this time of day. The water looks like blood. And your shadow—it looks as if you're bleeding to death on the sand.

(continued)

Name _____　Date _____

Imagery *(continued)*

Description 1

They had been walking through the forest for what seemed like hours. The thick canopy of leaves overhead blocked out all sight of the sun. In here, all was twilight. The air was hot, humid, motionless. Gradually, they realized that all the forest sounds had stopped. The clicks, squeaks, screeches of birds and other animals could no longer be heard. In the silence, their fear grew.

_____

_____

_____

_____

_____

_____

Description 2

Paula was led into the most beautiful room she had ever seen. Late-afternoon sunlight streamed in through what looked like dozens of floor-to-ceiling windows. The sheer drapes swayed in the gentle breeze as if dancing to the song of the birds outside. The ceiling was high, with complex scenes in white plaster against a glorious deep blue. As she crossed the carpet to the welcoming figure before her, Paula felt she had at last come home.

_____

_____

_____

_____

_____

_____

Name _____ Date _____

Imagery and Symbolism *(continued)*

Symbolism

A second way that dramatists, like poets, use images is to communicate ideas and feelings that can be understood on more than one level at the same time. This concentrated use of language can add great power to the experience of a drama.

Some words have more than one kind of meaning, or **denotation** and **connotation**. A word's denotation is its literal meaning. The denotation of the word "knife" is "a tool that cuts." A word's connotations include related ideas that might be associated with it. For the word "knife," the reader might associate such ideas as "blood," "violence," and even "murder."

Powerful examples of combined denotative and connotative meanings can often be found in titles. Like the titles of many short stories or novels, drama titles often contain both literal and symbolic ideas. These ideas may be important to the meaning of the drama.

Consider the title of the film *Jaws*. Besides its literal meaning, what other thoughts and feelings do you associate with the word? Combined with the advertisement image of the

shark swimming up from the deep to attack a swimmer, the title of the film instantly communicated a compelling sense of what the film was about.

Dramatists also use symbolism in their writing. A **symbol** is a real object that is used to represent an abstract idea.

In many drama plots, specific objects on stage take on symbolic meanings. For example, an American flag displayed on stage can symbolize the idea of patriotism.

Similarly, objects in a plot—such as a ring, gun, or piece of clothing—can take on symbolic meanings. The objects remind the audience of key ideas that are important to the plot's themes. Sometimes the same images and symbolic objects recur throughout a play, often changing meaning as the plot grows.

In Tennessee William's play *The Glass Menagerie*, Laura's collection of fragile glass animals is used symbolically. Near the end of the play, Laura dares to allow Jim to hold her favorite glass piece, a unicorn. Later, when they begin to dance, it is knocked off the table and is broken. The broken glass unicorn suggests both fragility and vulnerability.

Name _____   Date _____

 *Exercise 3.3*

Analyzing Effective Titles

Directions: In the space below, choose three play, film, or TV drama titles that contain an image you believe effectively relates to the meaning of the work as a whole.

First, underline the image in the title. Then, in your own words, write the *denotative* and *connotative* meanings of the image. Finally, explain how you believe this image makes the title particularly effective.

Title 1: _____

denotative meaning: _____

connotative meanings: _____

_____

This image is effective because _____

_____

Title 2: _____

denotative meaning: _____

connotative meanings: _____

_____

This image is effective because _____

_____

Title 3: _____

denotative meaning: _____

connotative meanings: _____

_____

This image is effective because _____

_____

*Drama: A Comprehensive Guide
to Dramatic Elements and Style*

Name _____ Date _____

 *Exercise 3.4*

Using Symbolic Objects in Drama

In this brainstorming activity, you and your classmates are asked to think of as many *different* ways that the object of **a ring** might be used symbolically by a dramatist in both serious and comic plots.

Directions: Work in groups of three students. Designate one member of your group to act as scribe to write down all of the brainstorm ideas generated by the group. Using the ideas below to get you started, try to come up with 12 more ideas of your own. When all groups are finished, compare your ideas together as a class.

* <u>comic</u>: man begins to be haunted by his deceased ex-wife the day he takes off his wedding ring

* <u>serious</u>: a mysterious ring brings out the "dark side" of every character in the plot who dares to put it on

1. _____

2. _____

3. _____

4. _____

5. _____

6. _____

7. _____

8. _____

9. _____

10. _____

11. _____

12. _____

*Drama: A Comprehensive Guide
to Dramatic Elements and Style*

Name _____   Date _____

Themes and Ideas

Many people believe the main task of drama is to get audiences to feel emotions. The most satisfying dramas, however, are designed to make audiences think as well as feel.

In addition to developing characters and dramatizing plot, well-written dramas also communicate powerful ideas. A **theme** is any universal subject or topic in a drama.

Common Dramatic Themes

Think about themes you see dramatized every day in plays, films, and television dramas.

Example	Good vs. Evil, Illusion vs. Reality, Free Will vs. Destiny, Justice vs. Mercy, etc.

Themes like these help audiences recognize the shared ideas that link a specific dramatic story to their own lives. Themes enable dramas to speak to audiences, century after century and from culture to culture.

The plot of Euripides' classical Greek tragedy, *Medea*, offers a good example. In essence, it is the story of a powerful, passionate woman. When her husband betrays her, her love turns to hate, and she seeks revenge. Although the drama was written 24 centuries ago, today's audiences still relate to its universal themes.

Drama of Ideas

Dramas of ideas are written to communicate ideas rather than to dramatize themes through realistic characters or plot. Such drama is intended to teach rather than to entertain. It is carefully constructed to stimulate audiences into thinking about important issues in new ways.

In the twentieth century, George Bernard Shaw was known for writing plays that made people look at the issues of his day. Shaw confronted audiences' conventional notions about such issues as the role of women in society, military heroism, and marriage.

Propaganda

In extreme cases, manipulation of an audience's thoughts and feelings is called propaganda. Drama is labeled as propaganda when it has been designed to stop audiences from thinking for themselves at all. Such dramas work to make audiences accept a certain opinion.

(continued)

Drama: A Comprehensive Guide
    to Dramatic Elements and Style

Name _____   Date _____

Themes and Ideas *(continued)*

Wartime is often a time when propaganda flourishes. A classic example is the German dictator Adolf Hitler's hiring of filmmaker Leni Riefenstahl to promote his rise to power. Perhaps the most famous propaganda film of all time is her film *The Triumph of the Will*. It combines powerful images, music, and narration to hypnotize viewers rather than to inspire rational, critical thinking.

Underlying Messages

Finally, a drama may not seem to have an explicit message, yet it may still communicate underlying messages. The plots of popular TV programs have been written primarily to entertain audiences rather than to communicate values. However, every time you watch a television police drama in which the criminal

gets punished at the end, the drama sends the message that crime does not pay.

Plots can contain hidden prejudices. Even the dramatist may not have been aware of these when composing the script. Dramas can communicate certain biases, such as "foreigners can't be trusted" or "the best-looking characters always win in the end." Unhealthy ideas about beauty, gender roles, and other cultural values can be reinforced through such hidden messages.

Of course, realistic drama (like real life) is three-dimensional. It is not just a structure in which to debate ideas or communicate values. Just as skilled dramatists present well-rounded characters, they also present all sides of issues. The impact on the audience is to make us wiser rather than more opinionated. We are left with a greater sympathy for the rich complexities of living.

Drama: A Comprehensive Guide
to Dramatic Elements and Style

Name _____   Date _____

 Exercise 3.5

Themes in Television Drama

Even the lightest comedy plots and action drama on television, as well as "serious" drama, explore universal dramatic **themes**.

Directions: To become more aware of the roles of themes in drama, keep a record of different themes you encounter in *one week* of TV watching and list them in the space below. When your list is complete, mark with a star those items that matter most to you. Share your list and preferences with your class.

- _____
- _____
- _____
- _____
- _____
- _____
- _____
- _____
- _____
- _____
- _____
- _____
- _____
- _____
- _____
- _____
- _____

Drama: A Comprehensive Guide
to Dramatic Elements and Style

Name _____   Date _____

 *Exercise 3.6*

Messages in Drama

Directions: Think about two plays, films, or TV dramas that you have seen that you believe were written to communicate a specific message. (For instance, a made-for-TV movie about the dangers of teen drug use.)

List the name of each drama and briefly retell its plot. Then tell what you believe to be the intended message and explain how the dramatist attempted to communicate this message within the drama.

Title 1: _____

Plot Synopsis:_____

_____

Message: _____

_____

How Included in Plot: _____

_____

_____

Title 2: _____

Plot Synopsis:_____

_____

Message: _____

_____

How Included in Plot: _____

_____

_____

Drama: A Comprehensive Guide
to Dramatic Elements and Style

Name _____   Date _____

Tragedy

Tragic drama is one of the most powerful of all dramatic forms. It has captured the imagination of dramatists from the classical Greeks to Shakespeare to contemporary times. There are many definitions of what makes a drama a tragedy. Most definitions share at least some common characteristics.

The Tragic Hero

First, tragic drama often centers on a **tragic hero**. This central character becomes caught in a dramatic conflict that eventually leads to ruin or death. Classical tragedy focuses on a central character who is noble and holds a high rank.

Example	Oedipus, the tragic hero in Sophocles' *Oedipus the King*.

Modern tragedy, on the other hand, more often focuses on ordinary people.

Example	Willy Loman, the traveling salesman in Arthur Miller's *Death of a Salesman*.

The Tragic Flaw

A second characteristic of tragic drama is that the tragic hero is usually at least partially responsible for his or her ruin. Tragic heroes are often strongly influenced by factors outside the character's control. Still, the tragic hero's downfall is seen to result from a **tragic flaw**. Personal characteristics, such as pride, greed, and rage, contribute to the tragic hero's destruction.

For instance, the downfall and death of Shakespeare's Macbeth results largely from his own choices and actions. It is his own ambition to be king, as well as his inability to stand up to his wife's strong ambitions for him, that leads to his murder of King Duncan and its tragic consequences.

The Tragic End

A third attribute that nearly all tragedies share is the way that tragic plots conclude. Think of the tragedies that you have read or seen on stage. How many of them end in spectacular acts of violence, bloodshed, and death?

Having realized that it is actually his *own* acts that have brought plague to his city, Oedipus puts out his own eyes near the end of *Oedipus the King*. Shakespeare's *Hamlet* ends with nearly all the major characters lying dead on stage. Willy Loman dies at the end of *Death of a Salesman* in a suicidal car accident.

Why Do We Watch Tragedy?

Yet, having considered some of the characteristics of form that tragedies share, an important question remains. If tragic drama always ends unhappily for the hero, why do audiences still enjoy watching tragedy?

The answer is that the effect of tragic drama on audiences is uplifting rather than depressing. Why?

(continued)

Name _____   Date _____

Tragedy *(continued)*

One explanation is that tragic drama often involves dramatic plots that evoke powerful emotions. It is stimulating for audiences to share in the grand passions of characters who are larger than life—even if the drama ends in their ruin.

A second explanation lies in the fact that, despite the larger-than-life qualities of tragic characters, viewers are able to identify with their situations. We may not make mistakes as large or suffer consequences as severe. Still, the feelings that tragic heroes experience—ambition, jealousy, greed, hate—are in some way common to us all.

Finally, tragic characters ask serious questions that parallel those that interest us. Tragedy deals with profound mysteries, such as the nature of fate, personal responsibility, and the ultimate meaning of life. The lessons that tragic heroes learn, even in ruin and death, broaden our own understanding of life.

Drama: A Comprehensive Guide to Dramatic Elements and Style

Name _____   Date _____

Exercise 3.7

Tragedy in Drama vs. Tragedy in Real Life

Directions: Make notes in the spaces below as to how you might answer each of the following questions. Then share your thoughts with other class members.

1. How does the way we use the term "tragic" in everyday life differ from how it is applied to drama? Would events that we call "tragic" in everyday life be considered tragedy on stage? Why or why not?

   _____

   _____

   _____

   _____

   _____

2. Think about three play, film, or television dramas that you have seen that had a sad ending. Would you call any or all of these dramas a "tragedy?" Why or why not?

   _____

   _____

   _____

   _____

   _____

   _____

3. It's clear that as audience members we react to tragic drama differently than when tragic circumstances occur in our own lives. Name a stage, film, or TV drama that you would consider to be a "tragedy."

   _____

   _____

   How is the experience of watching the events of this tragic drama different, for example, from witnessing a serious car accident? What emotions would each make you feel? How are they similar? How are they different?

   _____

   _____

   _____

   _____

   _____

*Drama: A Comprehensive Guide
to Dramatic Elements and Style*

Name _____   Date _____

 *Exercise 3.8*

Tragic Heroes Today?

Directions: Review the qualities of a **tragic hero** and the concept of a **tragic flaw** as described in the reading. Think about how these concepts might be applied to the life stories of real-life contemporary figures whose lives have ended in disaster or death: politicians, rock stars, film celebrities, etc.

Choose one such public figure whose life you know something about. Describe the circumstances of his or her downfall. Would you characterize this person as a "tragic hero"? Why or why not?

_____

_____

_____

_____

_____

_____

_____

_____

_____

_____

_____

_____

_____

_____

_____

_____

_____

_____

_____

*Drama: A Comprehensive Guide
to Dramatic Elements and Style*

Name _____ Date _____

Melodrama

Melodrama involves a dramatic conflict that is essentially serious rather than comic. Many of today's popular dramatic forms—murder mysteries, horror movies, soap operas, and Westerns—fall into the category of melodrama.

Strong Central Conflict

What are the characteristics of melodrama? First, melodrama plots most often involve a strong central conflict between forces that are recognized as "good" and forces that are recognized as "evil." Monster movies, such as *Godzilla* or *Jurassic Park*, provide good examples of plots that are melodramatic. Early in the drama a threat arises. Then the main characters spend the remainder of the plot trying to combat this threat.

Example	*Jurassic Park*—out-of-control dinosaurs *Jaws*—man-eating shark

External Conflict

Second, unlike tragic heroes, characters in melodrama do not generally struggle with forces within themselves. Most often, the dramatic conflict in melodrama is external, often against other characters who hold values that conflict with their own.

Example	*Star Wars*—Luke Skywalker, Han Solo, Princess Leia battle characters who oppose The Force.

Final Triumph

A third difference between tragedy and melodrama is that tragedy always ends unhappily for the major character. Melodrama, on the other hand, usually ends well for the main characters. They win in the end, rather than die. Melodrama heroes, such as the police characters in so many television crime dramas, face moments of life-threatening danger in each episode. Yet they always get through the tough spots to triumph at the end.

Dramatic Types vs. Complex Characters

A fourth difference is that the characters in melodrama are usually less developed than the tragic heroes of tragic drama. Characters in melodramas are often types, rather than complex characters. They stand for ideas, such as good or evil. In many classic Western melodramas, for example, the "good" guys wear white and the "bad" guys wear black. It is clear who the heroes and villains are. The audience knows how they are expected to feel about them.

Entertaining, not Thought-Provoking

Finally, whereas the thematic and emotional elements of tragedy are thought-provoking, melodrama is written mostly to entertain. Melodrama does not challenge audiences to think about the meaning of life. Melodrama plots are constructed to elicit strong, yet uncomplicated, emotions from the audience. The melodrama plot aims for thrills and theatrical excitement.

Name _____   Date _____

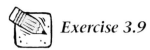 *Exercise 3.9*

Melodrama in Film and Television

Many popular film and television dramas fit the genre of melodrama as described in the reading.

Directions: From your own past viewing experience, choose *one* film drama and *one* television drama that you believe fits the category of melodrama.

Fill in the blanks below for each drama you have chosen. Be ready to explain to other class members *why* you believe these dramas fit the characteristics of melodrama.

Film Melodrama

Title: _____

Plot: _____

_____

Characters: _____

_____

Ending: _____

_____

Emotional impact on audience: _____

_____

Television Melodrama

Title: _____

Plot: _____

_____

Characters: _____

_____

Ending: _____

_____

Emotional impact on audience: _____

_____

Drama: A Comprehensive Guide
to Dramatic Elements and Style

Name _____ Date _____

Exercise 3.10

Invent Your Own Melodrama

Directions: Imagine that you have been hired as a scriptwriter to write an original drama for stage, film, or television that would fit into the dramatic genre of **melodrama**. First, review the characteristics of melodrama as described in the reading. Then, write a summary of your imagined melodrama including a possible **title**, a **plot summary** (including an account of the **central conflict** and the **climax**), and a detailed description of the major **characters**.

_____

_____

_____

_____

_____

_____

_____

_____

_____

_____

_____

_____

_____

_____

_____

_____

_____

_____

_____

_____

Name _____   Date _____

Comedy

Like tragedy, comic drama has traditions that can be traced back to the theater of the ancient Greeks. The conventions of comic drama are 24 centuries old. Comic dramatists have been "stealing" from their predecessors ever since.

Variations of the same comic plot situations can be traced from the classical Greek comedies of Menander all the way up to the twentieth century's silent film comedies, cartoons, and TV sitcoms!

Everyday Problems

In many ways, the conventions of comic and tragic drama are mirror opposites of each other. First, in contrast to the profound dramas of tragedy, comedy deals with much smaller everyday problems. These center around the complications of everyday life. Often, a specific problem emerges to be solved. Examples might be money to be found, a missing person, or a past injustice to be settled.

Comedy plots often center on complications involving romance.

Example	Shakespeare's *Much Ado About Nothing*—Beatrice and Benedick pretend to hate each other, end up in love

The Comic Hero

Second, whatever the plot conflict, comic heroes are quite different from tragic heroes. For one thing, the central characters in comedy are usually just ordinary folk. They are not royal or important.

Private Lives, **by Noel Coward**

(continued)

Drama: A Comprehensive Guide to Dramatic Elements and Style

Name _____ Date _____

Comedy *(continued)*

Further, the comic hero does not suffer from a tragic flaw. Comic characters are not perfect by any means, but their human qualities are accepted, not criticized.

Example	Bottom, from Shakespeare's *A Midsummer Night's Dream:* vain, boastful, arrogant—but appealing

A Happy Ending

A third contrast between comedy and tragedy is that the comic conflict always ends happily. Tragic heroes' lives end in ruin. Comic heroes do not suffer greatly. They end up as survivors, no matter how complicated the situations they have faced.

At the resolution of the plot, comic characters are punished for misdeeds only in proportion to their individual "crimes." No one dies. In fact, just as classical tragedy usually ends in death, classical comedy often concludes symbolically with a marriage celebration.

Example	Shakespeare's *As You Like It* ends with a multiple wedding

Think about all the comic plots you know—plays, films, or television dramas—that end with a wedding, or at least a kiss between significant characters. The final scene of a comedy often involves the reconciliation of characters who have been in conflict or the coming together of characters who have been falling in love all along.

Light-spirited Mood

Finally, in comparison with tragic drama, the mood of comedy is always high-spirited rather than solemn. However, the intention of comedy is often more than just to entertain. Comedy, like tragedy, can also deepen our understanding of life. Often the comic dramatist's intent is to show us a mirror image of ourselves. By getting us to laugh at humorous characters and situations, the playwright encourages us to recognize the comic side of our own human lives. The greatest comedic dramatists, such as Shakespeare and Molière, were able to teach us about ourselves while using laughter to help the medicine go down.

Name _____   Date _____

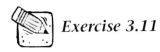 *Exercise 3.11*

Problems in Comedy

Directions: List six comedies, indicating whether they are plays or movies. Then identify the central problem in each.

Example	Comedy: *Ten Things I Hate About You* (movie)
	Central Problem: Patrick Verona has to get a date with Kit, a girl who claims to hate boys.

Comedy: _____

Central Problem: _____

_____

Comedy: _____

Central Problem: _____

_____

Comedy: _____

Central Problem: _____

_____

Comedy: _____

Central Problem: _____

_____

Comedy: _____

Central Problem: _____

_____

Comedy: _____

Central Problem: _____

_____

*Drama: A Comprehensive Guide
to Dramatic Elements and Style*

Name _____   Date _____

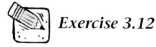 *Exercise 3.12*

The Comic Hero

Directions: Identify at least four comic heroes from plays, movies, or TV shows. Name the character's flaws. Then describe how audiences usually think of the character.

Example	Comic Hero: Lucy Ricardo, from *I Love Lucy* (TV show) Flaws: clumsy, gullible, inconsistent, scatterbrained Seen as: lovable ditz

Comic Hero:_____

Flaws: _____

Seen as: _____

Comic Hero:_____

Flaws: _____

Seen as: _____

Comic Hero:_____

Flaws: _____

Seen as: _____

Comic Hero:_____

Flaws: _____

Seen as: _____

Comic Hero:_____

Flaws: _____

Seen as: _____

Drama: A Comprehensive Guide
to Dramatic Elements and Style

Name _____   Date _____

Exercise 3.13

Create Your Own School Comedy Awards

Everyone has different tastes in humor. What seems funny to one person does not seem so to another.

Directions: Create a "Comedy Poll" to ask other students in your school about the comedies and comic actors that make them laugh.

You can interview other students personally and record their answers. Or you can distribute a sheet with questions on which they can write their own responses.

When all the results have been collected, tabulate the top scoring entries for each question and announce the winners to all those who have participated in your poll. Do you notice any interesting patterns in the results?

Some possible poll questions might include:

Favorite recent comic film:_____

Favorite current TV comedy: _____

Favorite current comic film actor: _____

Favorite current comic film actress: _____

Favorite current comic TV actor: _____

Favorite current comic TV actress: _____

Favorite current stand-up comedian:_____

Favorite comic film of all time: _____

Favorite TV comedy of all time: _____

Name _____   Date _____

 Exercise 3.14

Comedy as a Mirror

It has been said that the things that we laugh at can tell us important truths about ourselves. What do your personal favorite stage, film, and television comedies have to teach you about yourself?

Directions: Of all the recent stage, film, or television comedies that you have viewed, list your three favorite comedies below. Then, for each entry, list the specific elements of each comedy that you find to be most humorous, e.g., when the stuck-up opera singer got a pie in her face. Finally, suggest what this "comedy mirror" might reflect about you, e.g., "I don't like snobby people."

Title 1: _____

Elements that make me laugh: _____

_____

What these teach me about myself: _____

_____

Title 2: _____

Elements that make me laugh: _____

_____

What these teach me about myself: _____

_____

Title 3: _____

Elements that make me laugh: _____

_____

What these teach me about myself: _____

_____

Drama: A Comprehensive Guide
to Dramatic Elements and Style

Name _____   Date _____

Satire

Another type of drama falls somewhere between tragedy and comedy: **satire**. Satire is designed to educate viewers. It uses humor to expose corruption and abuse. For this reason, satire is often seen as being a special category of comedy, although satire always aims to do more than just entertain.

Calling Attention to Problems

Like tragedy and comedy, satire's history goes back to the ancient Greeks. Then and now, dramatists used satire to call attentions to problems in society and government. Satire presents a serious subject in a funny way. By showing the audience the ridiculous side of a subject, the satirist can help people look at things in a different way.

Example	Dario Fo's play *Can't Pay? Won't Pay!* is about a group of housewives who refuse to pay inflated prices for food. When it was first performed in England, it gave rise to a protest against paying the poll tax, a new tax that many people saw as unfair.

Everyday Problems, Exaggerated

The problems in satire are everyday problems. The setting of a satire is usually quite realistic. However, reality is often exaggerated. Just as a cartoonist may exaggerate a person's nose or eyebrows for comic effect, a satirist may exaggerate to make a problem obvious.

Example	The movie *Dr. Strangelove* was made in 1964. Its doomsday plot, with a madman giving the order to bomb Russia, was wildly unlikely. But it showed what *could* happen with the nuclear buildup and political distrust of the Cold War.

Some satires use gentle mockery to expose error and corruption. Some are bitter attacks. But all aim to serve the truth by exposing errors, in government and in society.

Example	Alain-René Lesage's play *Turcaret* was a biting satire on society. It showed people who were only motivated by greed and self-interest. The movie *The Gods Must Be Crazy* had a similar theme, but the satire was much gentler.

Drama: A Comprehensive Guide to Dramatic Elements and Style

Name _____   Date _____

 Exercise 3.15

Themes of Satire

Since satire aims to expose errors and corruption, different satires tend to address similar themes in politics and society.

Directions: Identify four pairs of satiric dramas that address the same theme. Say whether each drama is a play or a movie. Then describe the theme they both address.

Example	Drama 1: George Bernard Shaw, *Arms and the Man* (play)
	Drama 2: *Dr. Strangelove, or How I Learned to Stop Worrying and Love the Bomb* (movie)
	Common theme: The craziness of military buildup and war

Drama 1: _____

Drama 2: _____

Common theme: _____

Drama 1: _____

Drama 2: _____

Common theme: _____

Drama 1: _____

Drama 2: _____

Common theme: _____

Drama 1: _____

Drama 2: _____

Common theme: _____

Drama: A Comprehensive Guide
to Dramatic Elements and Style

Name _____   Date _____

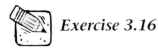 *Exercise 3.16*

Satire in Your Life

If you were going to use a play to point out a problem in society, what would it be? And how would you show the problem without lecturing an audience?

Directions: Identify a topic for a satire. It could be something in your local society or government, or something in world society or politics. Write one or two sentences describing the problem. Then describe how you could use humor to educate people about the problem.

Problem: _____

_____

_____

_____

_____

I could use humor to show this problem by:_____

_____

_____

_____

_____

_____

_____

_____

_____

_____

_____

Drama: A Comprehensive Guide
to Dramatic Elements and Style

Name _____ Date _____

Farce

Farce is the lightest and most playful of any of the categories of drama. Farce is actually a special category within the overall genre of comedy.

The most important dramatic element of farce is plot. More sophisticated comedy is built around fully developed comic characters. However, farce is built, first and foremost, on comic situations. Farce story lines are full of complications such as coincidences, mistaken identity, misunderstandings between characters, and more. Think about movie and television comedy plots that have involved exchanged briefcases, look-alike characters, or conflicts that occur when one character misinterprets another character's innocent action.

Second, the farce plot relies heavily on physical comedy: frenzied chases, doors opening and closing, hiding in closets, characters slipping on banana peels. Since its beginnings in the early part of the twentieth century, the medium of film has lent itself particularly to the physical comedy aspects of farce. The silent comedies of Charlie Chaplin and Buster Keaton always included hilarious chase scenes.

Example	In the movie *Mrs. Doubtfire,* plot complications force Robin Williams to keep changing in and out of his nanny costume.

A Flea in Her Ear, a French farce

(continued)

Drama: A Comprehensive Guide to Dramatic Elements and Style

Name _____   Date _____

Farce *(continued)*

Types, Not Full Characters

A third quality of farce is that it also relies heavily on type characters. Farce characters are not complex. Often specific physical or vocal characteristics are emphasized so that audiences know immediately how they are expected to react to each character.

Example	The aliens Tom, Dick, and Harry in the TV farce *Third Rock from the Sun*

Actually, the distinguishing mark of a truly successful farce is how the elements—comic situation, physical humor, character types—work together. The best farce plots are so carefully constructed that, once they are set in motion, nothing can stop them until the action runs its course. (It's interesting to note that farce shares this characteristic with classical tragedy.) From the very first moments, the dramatist begins to set up the comic combination of situation, characters, and physical setting. Farce then explodes into total chaos before all conflicts are ultimately resolved.

Aim to Entertain

Finally, the intention of farce is to entertain. The chief aim of farce, pure and simple, is fun. Farce does not try to communicate a message or to stir deep emotions. The goal of farce is to make us laugh—to celebrate the silliness of life.

Name _____ Date _____

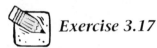 *Exercise 3.17*

Farce Humor in TV Sitcoms

Many TV situation comedies fall into the category of farce, often emphasizing frenzied plots, physical humor, and "type" characters.

Directions: Choose one episode of a favorite television comedy to study. During one episode of the program, count the number of studio audience laughs (or laughs on the "laff track") that are triggered by:

1. <u>situational humor</u> (e.g. a character having to hide in a closet)
2. <u>physical comedy</u> (e.g. funny facial expressions; falling down, etc.)
3. <u>verbal humor</u> (e.g. a character with a funny way of talking or wisecracking)

Record your Laugh Count results in the space below:

# of Situational:	
# of Physical:	
# of Verbal:	

Which type of humor is highest? How do your results compare with the findings of other students?

Name _____ Date _____

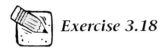 *Exercise 3.18*

The Role of "Type" Characters

Farce, like all comedy, often makes use of "type" characters. These supporting characters often have distinguishing physical or vocal characteristics and function in a number of ways in comic plots.

Directions: First, in the space below, brainstorm examples of "type" characters that appear in stage, film, and television comedies that you know. (One example might be the "nerd" characters that appear in so many teen film and TV comedies.)

_____

_____

_____

_____

_____

_____

When you are finished, share your list with the rest of the class. Discuss the various functions that these "type" characters serve in the plots in which they appear. In what ways do such characters add humor in themselves? For what other dramatic purposes do playwrights use them?

Part 4: Stage Tools—
Elements of Play Production

Objectives

1. To introduce students to the contributions of specific professionals involved in the stage production of a drama: the actor, the director, and other "behind-the-scenes" specialists;

2. To provide students with the opportunity of "trying out" production tasks related to the process of staging a play.

Teaching Tips

The "hands-on" activities suggested in this section (as well as other theater-related activities that you may create) can provide a way to "level the playing field" in your classroom, allowing non-academic students their moment to shine.

Look for ways to tap into the non-traditional intelligences and special gifts of your special needs students. Target students with acting or artistic talents who may not usually find themselves in school situations where they get to excel.

Warm-up Activity

Pursue contacts that you, a student in your school, or someone in your community may have to invite a theater professional—actor, director, scene designer, etc.—to visit your classroom and be interviewed by your class.

Have students prepare questions ahead of time for the visitor to answer. Questions could include asking about play productions that the guest has been involved with and

the specific contributions he or she made to them.

Other questions might include asking about how the visitor got started in his or her career. What advice could he or she give to interested students? What special training has the professional had to prepare for a career in the theater?

Extension Activities

- Reviewing a Stage Production: By the end of Part 4, students have been introduced to a wide range of critical concepts that should enable them to review a stage production from both a literary and production point of view. Refer students to Appendix B: **Tips for Reviewing a Dramatic Performance**.

- Careers in Drama: For students who are especially interested, these pages might serve as an introduction to more directed career-path investigations. Help interested students to find additional material from resources in your school and local library, the Internet, and theater professionals in your community.

- Advanced Acting Skills: Encourage students with an active interest in acting to read Constantin Stanislavski's famous work, *An Actor Prepares,* and to learn about the essentials of what has come to be called "method" acting. Perhaps a demonstration could be offered for the class.

(continued)

Part 4: Stage Tools—
Elements of Play Production *(continued)*

- <u>Advanced Directing Skills:</u> Students desiring more practice in scene blocking could be assigned a short dramatic scene to be staged with student actors for three different stage formats: 1) a proscenium stage, 2) a thrust stage, and 3) an arena stage ("theater in the round"). After the three stagings are performed for the class, have the student director explain staging choices that each stage format dictated.

Name _____ Date _____

The Actor's Tasks

The actor is the most visible of all the people involved in the production of a play. The success of any drama lies in the actors' ability to transform themselves realistically into the characters they are playing.

In any performance, an accomplished actor draws on many skills. Acting, like other professions, is a career that requires lifelong learning.

The Actor's Skills

Some of the actor's skills involve physical discipline, much like an athlete's training. Actors are often called upon to play characters who are physically different from themselves—older or younger, heavier or lighter. To develop the physical strength and flexibility necessary for taking on such roles, actors often study such disciplines as mime, modern dance, ballet, yoga, and fencing. By learning to be focused in body movement, they are more ready for the physical challenges of bringing any character realistically to life.

**Marcel Marceau,
French master of mime**

Another important set of acting skills involves the actor's voice. Actors practice vocal exercises to be able to project their voices on stage without microphones. Vocal exercises also help actors develop a broader vocal range. This allows them to express a full range of emotions in any role. Typically, voice training involves paying close attention to relaxation, breathing, and posture. It also involves techniques for producing specific voice sounds. Accomplished actors also master a variety of foreign language accents to allow them to play characters from different backgrounds. Most actors take singing lessons as well to be able to add singing to their repertoire of available skill.

In addition to physical and vocal training, actors need to exercise their intelligence. They are sometimes called on to memorize a great number of lines. These must be delivered perfectly, performance after performance. Actors must also develop a keen understanding of human nature. Alert actors are always studying people around them, as well as themselves. In their memory, they store away observations of small gestures, quirks of body language, and facial expressions. They build up a treasury of details to draw on when they develop a stage character. Actors must be good psychologists. They can only convincingly portray characters if they truly understand them from the inside.

Generally, actors do not instantly "become" the characters they play. Characters that they are assigned to play are "discovered" over time. Actors use two different processes to explore the character they are to play; many actors today draw on both techniques.

(continued)

*Drama: A Comprehensive Guide
to Dramatic Elements and Style*

Name _____   Date _____

The Actor's Tasks *(continued)*

Technique—the Outside-in Approach

The first process, which some actors call Technique, uses what might be called the outside-in approach. Actors using this approach start by concentrating on the externals of their characters. They put on the minutest details of their characters. In this way they teach themselves how to move and talk as their characters would.

Method—the Inside-out Approach

The second process, which some actors call Method acting, works from the inside out. Actors work first to discover the inner feeling of what it is like to be the character. The actor works to understand the character's background and motivations for behavior. Using Method, actors even begin rehearsals by ignoring the actual text of the play. They improvise (make up) scenes using invented dialogue of their own. Method actors may also draw on memories from times when they have experienced feelings similar to the character's. The Method process proposes that once an actor discovers a character from the inside, the outer physical details will be expressed automatically.

As a profession, acting is very competitive. For many actors just starting out, it takes a great belief in oneself just to audition for a part. It takes continued courage to handle the repeated rejection that actors must face waiting for the big break to come.

Richard III, Rustavalli Company, Georgia

Drama: A Comprehensive Guide
to Dramatic Elements and Style

Name _____   Date _____

Exercise 4.1

"Interview" Your Favorite Actor

You can learn more about the art of acting by finding out what celebrities themselves have to say about their craft and their own professional lives.

Directions: Choose an actor or actress (serious or comic) whom you admire. Think about what questions you would like to ask him or her if you were granted a personal interview. Some of your questions might include:

- What have been your favorite roles?
- What have been your least favorite roles?
- How did you get your start? Was getting started difficult?
- What training have you had? Are you still learning new skills?
- What are the best and worst things about being an actor?

Write at least five of your own additional questions here:

_____

_____

_____

_____

_____

_____

_____

_____

_____

_____

_____

Then, using resources from your library (books, periodicals, newspaper articles) and information found on Internet sites, research answers to your interview questions. Share your findings with your class.

Drama: A Comprehensive Guide
to Dramatic Elements and Style

Name _____ Date _____

 Exercise 4.2

Preparing and Presenting a Monologue

One strategy actors use to prepare performing a long speech is the script-marking method described below. Using such a technique will help you to better understand any text. It will also help with memorizing as well.

Directions: Ask your teacher to help you find a short monologue to prepare—either from a play that you have studied or perhaps from a book of monologues for actors. Then, follow the steps below.

1. First, slowly read the text out loud.

2. Next, read the text silently to yourself. Using a pencil, insert a double slash mark (//) to mark the major divisions of the text.

3. Next, read through the text again. This time, insert a single slash mark (/) to mark significant divisions within each section marked by a //.

4. Again read through the text. This time, underline (_____) key words and phrases that you believe should be emphasized when the text is performed. (Be careful not to underline too many.)

5. Read through the text again. This time, in the margin, write emotion cues—e.g. "sadly" or "getting angrier"—that you would like to emphasize at certain places throughout the text. (Draw a circle around them so that they stand out from the words of the text.)

6. Finally, read through the text one more time. This time, in the margin in brackets [ ], write stage directions—e.g. [slowly here] or [sit down]—as reminders as spots in the text.

Now, practice with your text aloud as marked, following the same directions each time you read it. You'll be surprised how easily it will become to perfect your delivery. Perform the prepared monologue for your class.

*Drama: A Comprehensive Guide
to Dramatic Elements and Style*

Name _____ Date _____

The Director's Tasks

In some ways, the director is like the CEO (Chief Executive Officer) of a large corporation. The director stands at the center of the great wheel of other people involved in a theater production. An effective director must possess a wide range of skills.

Head for Business

First, a director must have a head for business. Before a play begins production, the director works with the producer to develop a budget plan for the production. This budget includes salaries to pay the actors and other production crew members, the cost of building sets and costumes, advertising expenses, and much more.

Artistic Vision

A director must also have artistic vision. It is up to the director to determine the overall concept of the production, whether it is a play that has never been produced before or a play that has been produced previously. The director works with the scene designer, costume designer, lighting and sound designers, and others to coordinate a unified production.

Understanding of People

The director must know a great deal about human psychology and how to work with a wide range of personalities. In the audition process, for example, the director must make wise decisions in casting. The director must choose the best actor for each part. He or she must also put together an ensemble of actors who will work well together.

The director must continue to exercise people skills during the rehearsal process. The skilled director needs to know how to work with all of the personalities within a cast.

Early in rehearsals, the director must also script stage movements for each scene. This is referred to as "blocking." The director must keep the stage picture pleasing to the spectator's eye, as well as making certain that each character's movements fit his or her psychology.

Later on in the rehearsal process, the director helps the actors develop a deeper understanding of each scene. Then comes the task of adding costumes, props, and final sets in dress rehearsals.

In each of these steps, the director must function as crisis manager. It often falls to the director to help all the people involved cope with the tensions and stress of putting on a production.

Drama: A Comprehensive Guide to Dramatic Elements and Style

Name _____   Date _____

 *Exercise 4.3*

Creating a Director's Production Concept

Put yourself in the place of a director in the beginning stages of working out an overall concept for staging a play of your choice. Answer the questions below to get a feel for the kinds of creative choices a director must make.

Title of Play: (Choose a well-known play or an original work of your own.)

_____

Briefly Describe the Main Characters: _____

_____

List Settings Required: _____

_____

Name the Plot's Central Conflict(s): _____

_____

List Major Themes Dramatized: _____

_____

Does the Play Have a Prevailing Mood?: _____

_____

Sets, Costumes, and Makeup I Envision for this Production: _____

_____

_____

Types of Actors I Picture for This Production: _____

_____

Lighting and Sound Effects I Might Use: _____

_____

Drama: A Comprehensive Guide
to Dramatic Elements and Style

Name _____   Date _____

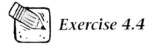 *Exercise 4.4*

Blocking a Stage Scene

"Blocking" is the process by which a director determines how characters are positioned on the stage and when and where they move. Follow the steps below to try your hand at the director's task of blocking a dramatic scene.

Directions

1. Ask your teacher to choose a scene from a play that your class has studied or choose a scene from a play that you have seen and read.

2. Read through the scene. Note where key dramatic moments occur in the scene. Also make note of places in the script where the author indicates specific actions or movements for characters.

3. On a large piece of paper or table top, layout a mock-up of the set as the playwright describes it or as you envision it. For instance, if the set includes doors, windows, or furniture, mark where they will be placed.

4. Use different colored pieces of paper to represent each character. Place them in position where they will be seen when the scene begins.

5. Slowly work through the scene line by line. Experiment with character placement and movements. At all times, think about what the overall stage picture will look like.

6. When you decide that a character should move—before, during, or after a line of dialogue, mark your script in pencil using these abbreviations:

   X = crosses to
   C = center stage
   US = upstage (away from the audience)
   DS = downstage (toward the audience)
   SL = stage left (from actor's point of view)
   SR = stage right (from actor's point of view)

7. When you have finished preparing your own blocking script, recruit student volunteers to walk through the scene in a space that approximates the size of the actual set. Make adjustments to your blocking script as necessary.

An interesting variation of this activity might be to have other class directors work with student casts of their own to stage the same scene and then compare the results. What directorial choices are similar? What choices are quite different?

Drama: A Comprehensive Guide
to Dramatic Elements and Style

Name _____   Date _____

Other Personnel of Stage Production

The production of any play involves a number of theater professionals who contribute their talents behind the scenes.

Producer

The producer (or team of producers) is in charge of the financial aspects of producing a play. The producer often chooses the play to be produced, then looks for funding to mount the production. Sometimes financial backing comes from private investors who are called, in theater slang, "angels." The producer often hires the director, who may share in further financial decisions regarding the production.

Stage Manager

The stage manager acts as assistant to the director. The stage manager acts as the eyes and hands for the director, helping communicate the director's wishes to other members of the production staff. One task of the stage manager is to mark down blocking decisions as they are finalized in rehearsals. Another role is to be "on book" (reading the script) so that actors may ask for a line during later rehearsals when they have stopped carrying their own scripts.

Scene Designer and Stage Carpenter

The scene designer works with the director to design stage settings that fit the director's concept for the overall production. The scene designer's set designs play a major role in helping to create the mood and atmosphere of the stage setting. They also define the playing spaces in which the actors will act. Once a design concept

is agreed upon, the scene designer draws up plans which are then given to the stage carpenter and assistants to build.

Lighting Designer

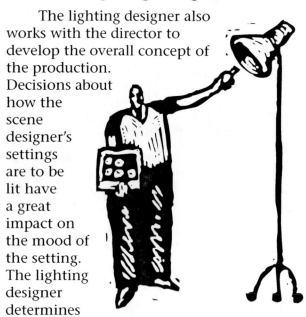

The lighting designer also works with the director to develop the overall concept of the production. Decisions about how the scene designer's settings are to be lit have a great impact on the mood of the setting. The lighting designer determines which areas of the stage will be lit, as well as how brightly and by what colors. During each performance, a lighting technician manages the lighting board, following cues marked on the lighting script.

Sound Designer

The sound designer is in charge of providing the recorded sounds, as well as live sound effects, that are necessary for the production. A sound technician follows the stage action during each performance. He or she provides sound cues such as a telephone ringing, doorbell chimes, recorded music, and glass crashing.

(continued)

Name _____ Date _____

Other Personnel of Stage Production *(continued)*

Costume Designer

The costume designer follows the director's vision for how the costumes should look. The costumes must fit the themes of the production, as well as fit the time period of the setting and the character they are designed for. Costumes must also be coordinated with the color scheme and overall "look" of the scene design, especially its color scheme. During each performance, the costume designer or members of the costume staff may be on hand to help actors with quick costume changes.

Property Master

The property master is in charge of gathering props (short for "properties") for the production. Props include those items that are held by actors, such as newspapers, hunting rifles, or musical instruments. Props also include furniture and set dressings that are used to decorate the settings, such as armchairs, books in a bookshelf, fireplace utensils, etc. During each performance, the property master and stage assistants manage the scene changes.

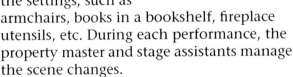

Makeup Artist

The makeup artist oversees the design of makeup for the entire production. When necessary, the makeup artist teaches actors how to apply makeup appropriate for the specific characters they play. Character parts may require extras such as false moustaches or beards made of crepe hair, putty noses, or wigs. The makeup artist and crew may also help actors prepare for each performance.

Support Personnel

The production staff employs a variety of support personnel. Box office employees oversee the sale of tickets. Publicity and public relations people oversee advertising as well as inviting critics to attend and review performances. At performance times, the house manager oversees ushers and refreshment sellers.

Name _____   Date _____

 Exercise 4.5

Review the Production Elements of a Performance

When professional critics review a dramatic performance, they tend to focus on the quality of the play itself or the actors' performances. If production elements are mentioned at all, they usually take second place.

Directions: To reverse the usual trend, attend a live theater performance and write a review that focuses primarily on the work of those behind-the-scenes professionals who have contributed so much to the overall production. As you watch the performance, jot notes in the appropriate columns below:

Scene Design: _____

_____

_____

Lighting Design: _____

_____

_____

Sound Design: _____

_____

_____

Costume Design: _____

_____

_____

Stage Properties: _____

_____

_____

Makeup Design: _____

_____

_____

Drama: A Comprehensive Guide
to Dramatic Elements and Style

Name _____ Date _____

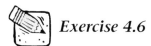 *Exercise 4.6*

Designing for the Theater

The theater uses the talents of professionals with a wide range of design skills. Even if you do not consider yourself an artist, have some fun exploring one or more of the design activities listed below.

- **Graphic Arts:** Choose a well-known or original play and design a "logo" to be used for promoting an upcoming production. Often such a logo is used for newspaper and billboard advertising, the program cover, and possibly for merchandise related to the production such as T-shirts.

- **Set Design:** Choose a well-known or original play and design a set (or sets) for an upcoming production. Work in any medium you wish: sketch, watercolor, blueprint, or three-dimensional constructions. Be sure to note what kind of stage your design is intended for: amphitheater, proscenium, thrust stage, or arena (theater-in-the-round).

- **Costume Design:** Choose a well-known or original play and work up costume design illustrations for an upcoming production. Try to work in a medium that includes color. If the play is a period piece, you will need to research the clothing of that era. Remember, too, that classic plays can be creatively staged in any era, so feel free to use your imagination.

- **Makeup Design:** Makeup design is a skill that must be learned from other professionals. If you are interested in this area, look for books about makeup design in local libraries or speak to theater professionals in your community. Try to get access to some hands-on makeup supplies and experiment with making up yourself and/or friends. Take pictures of results that please you and share them with your class.

Drama: A Comprehensive Guide
to Dramatic Elements and Style

Appendix A: Drama Vocabulary

antagonist the character in a drama who opposes the main character

climax the point in a drama when the conflict comes to a head

complication a new element introduced into the plot that affects the course of action of the drama

conflict the central tension on which the action of a drama is built; conflict can be *between characters, between a character and outside forces, within a character,* or a *mixture* of these different types

connotation any non-literal meaning associated with an image

denotation the literal meaning of a word

dramatic unity the quality of having all the actions of a drama relate logically to the central conflict

exposition the means by which a playwright communicates background information about characters and plot to the audience

farce a genre of drama that involves a "comic" dramatic conflict, but aims more to entertain than to introduce sophisticated comic themes

imagery descriptive language that makes use of similes or metaphors

melodrama a dramatic genre like tragedy that involves a "serious" dramatic conflict but aims more to entertain than to explore deeper tragic themes

plot the "story" of the drama; the structure of important events that occur during the course of the play

point of attack the moment in the plot when the chain of events of the drama is set in motion that leads eventually to the *crisis* and *resolution*

protagonist the leading character in a drama, opposed by the *antagonist*

resolution the end of the drama, containing the final solution to the conflict

satire a genre of drama that uses comedy to expose social and political ills

setting the environment in which the drama takes place; setting places the action in a specific place and time, contributes to the mood, and reflects the psychology of the characters

subtext the underlying message communicated when characters express one idea but are really thinking or feeling something else

symbol a real object that is also used to represent an abstract idea

theme any universal topic represented in a drama that gives it structure or focus

tragic flaw an element of the tragic hero's own character that contributes to his or her tragic downfall

tragic hero the central character in a tragedy, who becomes caught in a dramatic conflict that leads to his or her own ruin or death

Appendix B:
Tips for Reviewing a Dramatic Performance

Whether you are viewing a stage play, film, or television production, learning the steps to reviewing a dramatic performance will help you experience any drama more fully and enjoy it more.

A good critic is knowledgeable about what makes effective drama. To review a performance effectively, you will have to rely on concepts you have learned about the elements of drama. Before critiquing a performance, take time to review all readings and student worksheets you have worked on. Make a note of any concepts that you have questions about and share them with your teacher.

Good critics also pay careful attention to their own responses to the performance they are reviewing. Be aware of the different emotions you feel throughout the performance. When do you get caught up in the action? When are you bored? At what moments do you feel special sympathy for the characters and their situation?

Be honest. If the performance did not move you, say so. But try also to say *why* you think it failed to do so. If you liked the performance very much, try also to get beyond vague praise; tell *why* you liked it— as precisely as you can. No two critics will review a performance in exactly the same way, but all good critics support their opinions with specific evidence from the performance.

Even viewing an unsatisfying drama doesn't have to be a waste of time. At the very least, thinking carefully about what factors contribute to a "bad" drama can teach you more about what makes "good" drama good.

There are a number of strategies for improving your skills as a reviewer. One important technique is to expose yourself to reviews of established professional reviewers. Collect theater, film, and TV reviews from newspapers and magazines that are available to you.

Since reviews also are broadcast on non-print media, such as radio and television, pay attention to these review sources as well. If you find critics whom you especially like, try recording reviews from radio or TV to analyze and even copy.

If possible, compare reviews of the same drama from a number of sources. Then "review" the reviews. Which reviews do you think are best? Why? What can they teach you about developing your own reviewing style?

Finally, to improve the quality of your reviewing, try keeping a "reviewer's journal." Record your own personal reactions to a variety of dramatic performances (stage, film, television) that you view, perhaps over the period of a month or more.

(continued)

Appendix B:
Tips for Reviewing a Dramatic Performance *(continued)*

Be as personal in your reactions as you can be. Carefully write down your honest responses to what you view. Remember to apply, whenever possible, concepts about the elements of drama that you have learned about in class.

Now read through the Checklist for Reviewers. This checklist will provide you with ideas for reviewing (or even just viewing) any dramatic performance—whether on stage, film, or television.

Be sure to read through the checklist *before* viewing a performance. Then refer to the checklist again *afterwards* to guide you while writing your review.

You may wish to share your review(s) with your class. An interesting activity might be to have each class member view the same dramatic performance and then compare reviews with those of other students.

Checklist for Reviewers

I. Before Viewing the Performance—Prepare

- Be rested, relaxed, and ready to be alert.

- Keep an open mind. Don't decide ahead of time what you will like or dislike.

- *Before* the performance, review the questions listed in Section II to help you focus.

- Carry a small notebook or pad to take notes during the performance.

II. While Viewing the Performance—Apply Ideas You Have Learned

A. Evaluate the Dramatic Structure

- Is the central conflict powerful? Does it hold your attention throughout?

- Is the plot logical? Does it develop the central conflict?

- Are the characters well-developed? Are they believable? Do you care about them and the conflicts they face?

- Is the dialogue effective? Is it true to life? Does it express the characters well?

- Is the setting well-established? Does it contribute to the drama in significant ways?

- Does the drama use images and symbols in significant ways? Do they add to the impact of the drama?

- Does the drama explore interesting themes? Are they relevant to your own life situation?

- How does the drama fit into the dramatic genres of tragedy, melodrama, comedy, or farce?

B. Evaluate the Production

- Is the performance well-paced? Is it slow or hard to follow in places?

- Does the acting move you? Are there times when it is not believable?

- Do the scene design, lighting, costume design, and other production elements add to the performance in significant ways?

- Does sound or music play a significant role?

C. Evaluate the Audience's—and Your Own—Response

- When does the audience seem most involved? Make a note of the moments when you *most* enjoy the performance.

- When does the audience seem bored? Make a note of moments when you *least* enjoy the performance.

(continued)

Checklist for Reviewers *(continued)*

III. When Writing Your Review—Be Specific

- Take a stand. Decide on your own point of view.

- Be honest. State and defend your personal opinion. Don't be swayed by what you believe others think or feel.

- Support your opinions with specifics from the performance. Review your notes.

- Use drama vocabulary words in your review. Try to apply the concepts you have learned in your review.

Appendix C:
Playscript Format and Playscript Sample

Playscript Format

Describe the **setting** of your play here. Where and when does the play take place? Give the basics about scenery, furniture, and objects that appear on stage. *Write this description single spaced on the right half of the page.*

(The opening stage directions go here—often beginning with a phrase like "AS THE LIGHTS COME UP" or "AS THE CURTAIN RISES." Tell us WHO is on stage and what they are doing. You can also describe what they look like. *Always type character names in CAPITALS. Enclose stage directions in parentheses.*)

[*Type the character's name—in CAPS—centered above each speech*]

CHARACTER A

Write the words that CHARACTER A speaks here. [*Notice that you do not use quotation marks as you would if you were writing fiction.*]

CHARACTER B

Write here the words that CHARACTER B says back to CHARACTER A. [*Notice that speeches are typed single spaced.*]

CHARACTER A

[If you choose, you can tell the actor <u>how</u> to say the speech. *Put these directions in italics and within parentheses.* For example:]

(*Angrily*) Then, write the speech that follows.

(Whenever you want to indicate some particular action on the stage, insert stage directions *in parentheses.* Describe what you want to see happen on the stage.)

[If a character's speech is interrupted by an action, set it up like this . . .]

CHARACTER B

Beginning of character's speech here . . .

(Stage action described—*in parentheses*—here)

Continue and conclude character's speech here.

Playscript Sample

A teenage girl's bedroom. Furniture includes a single bed, telephone on an endtable, a rocking chair and reading lamp, and a small desk. Posters of favorite movie celebrities on the wall.

(AS LIGHTS COME UP, JULIA is lounging on the bed and talking on the phone. Dressed in clean, stylish sweatclothes, she is 15 years old, pretty and full of life.)

JULIA

I can't believe he said that to her! Really??? . . . I would NEVER allow Randy to speak to me that way . . .

(There is a knock on the bedroom door. JULIA ignores it.)

Then what did <u>she</u> say?

(There is another knock, a bit more insistent.)

(*In an irritated, sing-song tone*) I'm on the <u>pho-one</u> . . .

(MOM opens the door tentatively. She is in her mid-forties, wearing an apron. She looks very distressed.)

MOM

Julia, I'm sorry to interrupt—but I need to talk to you right away.

JULIA

(*Speaking into phone*) I guess I gotta go, Sarina. I'll call you back in a while.

(*Glaring at her mother*) So what's so important it couldn't wait?

(MOM comes into the room and sits quietly on the side of JULIA'S bed.)

MOM

(*Finding it hard to speak*) Honey, there's something I need to tell you.

(JULIA sits up in bed as she senses something serious.)

It's about Randy. He's . . . been in an accident. [*THE SCENE CONTINUES* . . .]

Drama: A Comprehensive Guide to Dramatic Elements and Style

Appendix D:
Screenplay Format and Screenplay Sample

Screenplay Format

EXT. [or INT.] PLACE OF SCENE—DAY [or NIGHT]

Describe the **setting** of the scene here—*single spaced.* [*"EXT." means EXTERIOR; "INT." means INTERIOR*] What does the camera see? What do the surroundings look like? Any **SOUNDS?**—*capitalize.* What **CHARACTERS**—*capitalize*—are present? What do they look like? What are they doing?

If you choose, you can also indicate specific **CAMERA INSTRUCTIONS** in your screenplay script. A few common camera instructions include:

<u>LONG SHOT</u> (LS)	a shot photographed from a distance
<u>CLOSE UP</u> (CU)	a person or object photographed up close
<u>MEDIUM SHOT</u>(MS)	a shot midway between a long shot and closeup
<u>AERIAL SHOT</u>	a shot from high above—from a plane or helicopter
<u>ZOOM SHOT</u>	when the camera zooms in from a distance
<u>PAN SHOT</u>	when the camera swings right or left on a fixed base
<u>DOLLY SHOT</u>	the camera moves along the ground on wheels

MEDIUM SHOT—CHARACTER A AND CHARACTER B
[*this is an example of a possible **camera instruction**]*

CHARACTER A

[indent . . .] Tell what CHARACTER A says here—*single spaced.*

You can interrupt a character's speaking—or insert directions <u>between</u> character speeches—to describe [*single spaced*] **character actions** that take place and/or **camera instructions** that tell how you want the action to be photographed.

CLOSE UP—CHARACTER B

CHARACTER B

[indent . . .] Tell what CHARACTER B replies here.

Continue to describe any **character actions** or **camera instructions** as described above.

CHARACTER C (V.O.)

["V.O."—**Voice Over**—indicates that the character's voice is heard, but the character does not appear on screen, such as used for **narration**.]

[indent . . .] Tell what CHARACTER C says here . . .

To indicate the **end of the scene,** *write in the right-hand margin:*]   CUT TO:

EXT. [or INT.] PLACE OF <u>NEXT</u> SCENE—DAY [or NIGHT] [etc.]

Drama: A Comprehensive Guide
to Dramatic Elements and Style

Screenplay Sample

EXT. MOUNTAIN ROAD—DAY
AERIAL SHOT of a pickup truck racing up a winding mountain road—being chased by a police car. We hear sounds of MOTORS RACING and TIRES SQUEALING. Camera ZOOMS in on the pickup.   CUT TO:

INT. PICKUP TRUCK—DAY
In the driver's seat is ROLLO, 50's, overweight, unshaven, dressed in a dirty work shirt and jeans. In the passenger seat is SLIM, early 20's, wearing a clean white tee-shirt and khaki shorts, smoking nervously.

CLOSE-UP—SLIM
He is looking through the truck's rear window at the police car behind them.

                              SLIM

     They're gaining on us, Rollo! Can't you go any faster?

CLOSE-UP—ROLLO
He glances casually through the driver-side rear-view mirror.

                             ROLLO

     Don't sweat it, kid. We'll outsmart them at the bridge.   CUT TO:

INT. POLICE CAR—DAY
In the driver's seat is JACK FLASH, 35 and handsome. In the passenger seat is PETE MULDOON, early 60's and seasoned. Both are dressed in uniform. From the start, it is clear that the men have worked together as a team for years.

                            MULDOON

     They're probably going to pull something funny at the bridge, Pete.

                             FLASH

     It's already covered, old man. I radioed ahead for backup ten minutes ago.   CUT TO:

EXT. MOUNTAIN ROAD—DAY
Both vehicles speed ahead up the mountain road—offscreen left—as the Camera PANS right to view the desert valley below.

                         MULDOON (V.O.)

     And so another day of duty with my partner begins . . .   CUT TO:

Appendix E:
Recommended for Further Reading

The books listed below offer a sampling of publications available today on a range of topics related to theater arts.

Some of the older texts listed have become "classics" in the field. Most of the more recent listings are available in inexpensive paperback editions.

Acting

- Barr, Tony. *Acting for the Camera*. HarperCollins, 1997.
- Boleslovsky, Richard. *Acting: The First Six Lessons*. Theater Communications Group, 1933.
- Hagen, Uta and Frankel, Haskel. *Respect for Acting*. IDG Books Worldwide, 1979.
- Meisner, Sanford. *Sanford Meisner on Acting*. Vintage Books, 1987.
- Stanislaviski, Constantine. *An Actor Prepares*. Theater Arts Books, 1936.
- Strasberg, Lee. *A Dream of Passion: The Development of Method*. New American Library, 1990.

Stage Directing

- Clurman, Harold. *On Directing*. Fireside, 1997.
- Converse, Terry John. *Directing for the Stage: A Workshop Guide of 42 Creative Training Exercises and Projects*. Meriwether Publications, 1995.
- Desrochers, Rick. *Playing Director—A Handbook for Beginners*. Heinemann, 1995.
- Reid, Francis. *The Staging Handbook*. Heinemann, 1996.
- Taylor, Don. *Directing Plays*. Theater Arts, 1997.

Stage Design

- Ingham, Rosemary. *From Page to Stage: How Theater Designers Make Connections Between Scripts and Images*. Heinemann, 1998.
- Lounsbury, Warren C. *Theater Backstage from A to Z*. University of Washington Press, 2000.

Costume Design

- Jackson, Sheila. *Costumes for the Stage: A Complete Handbook for Every Kind of Play*. New Amersterdam Books, 1990.
- Kidd, Mary T. *Stage Costume Step-By-Step*. Betterway Publications, 1996.

(continued)

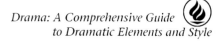
Drama: A Comprehensive Guide to Dramatic Elements and Style

Appendix E:
Recommended for Further Reading *(continued)*

Playwriting and Screenwriting

- Egri, Lajos. *The Art of Dramatic Writing.* New York: Simon & Schuster, 1977.
- Field, Syd. *Screenplay: The Foundations of Screenwriting.* Dell Books, 1984.
- Hunter, Lew. *Lew Hunter's Screenwriting 434.* Berkeley, 1994.
- King, Viki. *How to Write a Movie in 21 Days: The Inner Movie Method.* HarperCollins, 1988.
- Root, Wells. *Writing the Script: A Practical Guide for Films and Television.* Henry Holt, 1987.
- Seger, Linda. *Creating Unforgettable Characters.* Henry Holt, 1990.
- Seger, Linda. *Making A Good Script Great: A Guide for Writing and Rewriting.* Samuel French, 1994.

Share Your Bright Ideas with Us!

We want to hear from you! Your valuable comments and suggestions will help us meet your current and future classroom needs.

Your name_____Date_____

School name_____Phone_____

School address_____

Grade level taught_____Subject area(s) taught_____Average class size_____

Where did you purchase this publication?_____

Was your salesperson knowledgeable about this product?   Yes_____   No_____

What monies were used to purchase this product?

____School supplemental budget   ____Federal/state funding   ____Personal

Please "grade" this Walch publication according to the following criteria:

Quality of service you received when purchasing .... A   B   C   D   F

Ease of use.. A   B   C   D   F

Quality of content.. A   B   C   D   F

Page layout .... A   B   C   D   F

Organization of material .... A   B   C   D   F

Suitability for grade level .... A   B   C   D   F

Instructional value.. A   B   C   D   F

COMMENTS:_____

_____

What specific supplemental materials would help you meet your current—or future—instructional needs?

_____

Have you used other Walch publications? If so, which ones?_____

May we use your comments in upcoming communications?   ____Yes   ____No

Please **FAX** this completed form to **207-772-3105**, or mail it to:

Product Development, J. Weston Walch, Publisher, P.O. Box 658, Portland, ME 04104-0658

We will send you a **FREE GIFT** as our way of thanking you for your feedback. **THANK YOU!**